Prophetic Poetry

Prophetic Poetry

Holy Agitation for Peace, Justice, and Passion

RONALD L. FAUST

RESOURCE *Publications* • Eugene, Oregon

PROPHETIC POETRY
Holy Agitation for Peace, Justice, and Passion

Resource Publications
An Imprint of Wipf and Stock Publishers
199 W. 8th Ave., Suite 3
Eugene, OR 97401
www.wipfandstock.com

ISBN 13: 978-1-60899-097-9

Manufactured in the U.S.A.

K

Contents

Author's Preface

POETRY OFFERS THE LANGUAGE of the heart. So much of life is like lawn mowing, maintaining a steady drone of patterns back and forth, leveling down the feeble little stalks of grass, and filling our time with a predictable operation of cutting machines and surveying our work with a satisfied sense of pride. It's left brain work. Predictable. Poetry is right brained. Intuitive. Using words to catch the imagination. It's another way to capture reality deeper than the surface of our senses.

So much of life on a larger scale has produced weapons of destruction. Suddenly it is normal to believe that we can only be safe if we have bigger weapons than the next guy. We have transferred the playground of the bully into toys that have the potential of destroying all living things. We have normalized a world of fear by surrounding ourselves with our idolization of the work ethic, believing that we need jobs for our economy yet it doesn't matter if what we produce harms us. Others would say this leads to insane thinking. What we think is normal may need something abnormal to shake us out of this lethargy of plastic robotic zombie-ism. Left brain thinking doesn't understand poetry. Because of this, poetry is precisely what is required.

I love poetry. The language of the soul reaches deeper than spending my days mowing my lawn or wondering how my nation will control the destiny of others. It's taken me a little time to free up my poetry and maybe it still is a little tight with the need to rhyme and fit into patterns of predictability. But I have come around to appreciate free verse and the attempt to catch the right word and the right thought in the right place with a "left" slant, because poetry ought to be iconoclastic.

This is why we call this Prophetic poetry. Many do not know what this means, and they fall into some drivel about predicting the end times or something about being sentimental and emotional about nation, God and faith. The prophetic function comes up against and makes corrections upon the establishment. In the church a priestly function preserved the sacraments but the protestant tradition came out to drive a protest against certain abuses. It relied on a long trail of prophets who like Jeremiah railed against war and nation or like Isaiah lifted up advocacy for a higher vision of hope. The Prophets gave us our best understanding of God, which elevated our notion of a loving compassionate energetic Creator. The poetry in this anthology asks some tough questions about how we are doing, what is our significance, and why we are going down a path that can lead to destruction.

So often the cacophony of faith and national voices are not hearing each other, so that poetic voices are dismissed by pragmatists. If we could only pause and listen—and not just use scripture to bolster a particular point of view to become defensive about war for instance, but to see the sweep of faith as people on the move, sojourners for peace, seekers of a gentler path. Likewise, poetry needs to stay grounded in justice work, what's fair, what levels the playing field, what balances the head and heart.

This book could be about poems of peace. Justice concerns such as immigration and poverty issues are here as well, interconnected. Time and space offer occasions for the poetic spark, but sometimes poetry is just a healthy outlet for our righteous indignation. We need poets to lift up values of importance, such as this sample from the book describing peacemakers.

> Maybe peacemakers are like insurgent poets,
> Irrelevant, dissident, disregarding the status quo,
> Imagining a vision of a world that gets along
> When "staying the course" is not the way to go.

Poetry dares us to break free from safe-boxed thinking. Poetry becomes an agent of transformation in offering a new direction for our lives. It requires a little holy agitation by tossing poems like pebbles into placid pools of water to cause some waves. Such poetry gives us prophetic alerts to pay attention to what is most important, like peace not war, like fairness not control, like the values of universal church not parading hypocrisy, like advocacy for the poor not selfishness.

In 2009 the poems recognize a shift of consciousness, that we had conservative leadership trying to conserve tradition before giving way to liberal voices, more open, more susceptible to change. This shift in history was noted as a Biblical phrase "creation of the new," one of those two score surges in the poetic energy of the human experiment.

Some of my best writing has to do with passion in describing the yin-yang tension of life and what keeps us alive to each day. I prefer poetry of tension that tweaks my interests and juices my passions. And we need someone to listen and share our life's journey. Thanks to my wife, Toni, and also those who participated in this poetry project, such as Jonne Long who provided editing assistance. The "On occasions" at the bottom of each poem are not aids to overanalyze the poem but opportunities for creating new participation in the events. I confess some per"verse" pleasure in plunging the word deep into the pool of dialogue to bob up to the surface of shared learning. Again it takes a village to raise an enlightened book.

We all pick ultimate concerns, sometimes as substitutes for God's love, but the human being seems restless until persons find a satisfyingly adequate and more authentic expression of their significance. The poetry here assists us in giving voice to a spiritual reality in our desire for meaning and passion and creativity and wisdom and love. Agitate and enjoy.

PART ONE

Peacemaking

Shalom be with you

Peace I leave with you; my peace I give to you;
not as the world gives do I give to you.
Let not your hearts be troubled,
neither let them be afraid.

JOHN 14:27

1

Bullets Fail–Let Peace Prevail

How strange the fascination with bullets,
Hard, brassy, classy, shiny in their cases,
Poised, coiled in the chambers of weapons,
    Until triggered, flying through fleshy places.

How foolish are the grabbers who rein in others,
    Powerful, like pro-wrestlers, except with a gun,
Strutting, cajoling, suppressing, acting big,
    Passing on a macho mask from father to son.

People may work, picking up a paycheck,
    Never once having to ask who's to blame,
When a sixteen year old boy finds a gun,
    Targets his school as if on a video game.

Nobody knows where goes those bullets,
    Maiming a soldier, trying not to die in vain,
But killing another, nobody really cares,
    How the violence makes us all go insane.

And so the bullets travel through Iraq,
    Fighting a wretched war built on a lie,
Or into the scary scenes of street gangs
    Fighting for recognition before they die.

So many bully bullets roam around the world,
    Tearing apart the beauty of innocent's delight,
To crumble the walls that keep them out
    And steal the scarce little that is their right.

When will we ever learn that bullets hurt
    Our chances to make life our ultimate goal,
Because, before the flame of love flickers out,
    We must nurture peace or rip apart our soul.

    (On the occasion of the 4th Anniversary of the Iraq war, March 1, 2007)

Bush and Nixon in Limbo

Both were impeached, except one escaped,
Avoiding the horror of war,
Denying the climate crisis,
    Hiding the struggle of the poor,

Yet both blended a commonality for war,
    Protecting the rich and powerful
Raising support for the military
And bankrupting the economy,

While both found liberals to blame
And lied to maintain their cover up,
    That they were tough empire Presidents
As others back bended under limbo bars.

    It took an interminable hell of a time,
To endure their dim witted destructiveness,
Yet what is so amusing about low limbos
Are the sorry bimbos who revere their memory.

    (On occasion of wondering how low we can go during the Bush era)

Call 911

Unspeakable strangulated silence
     Lingers in the echo chambers
Of our hollow hearts, congested
     By the layered cholesterol
Of fatty white lies,
     That it was Sadaam or Osama
Who were the cause of all our problems,
After two airliners collide
With two titan towers
Bringing the financial goliaths
To their knees, collapsing
The impenetrable veneer
     That any one nation has a right
To lord it over many other nations.

     911 was a call for help,
but arrogant and deaf leaders missed the call,
too proud to admit that nations need help,
more prone to blame anyone else
and name calling them "terrorist,"
a perfect substitute for old enemies,
the communists—a worthy monster,
in which to spread high alert fear
and divert the money making machine
behind secret doors—to sell bullets
and steal oil and build empire,
    looking more and more
     like we become the actual terrorists
to the rest of a desperate world.

     If only we had listened
Instead of starting Bush's war.
Maybe we would not have caused
     Our own heart attack
As a nation, collapsing

Into an evil vortex of tornadic destruction,
Call 911 for emergency rescue and
Help us to learn from Viet Nam,
     That more war causes more pain,
That only a confession of wrong

Will heal our soul, finding "We" instead of me,
That national pride gets in the way
     Of rest and exercise,
     For finding our soul
        through peace and justice,
Most assuredly, we could die or get better,
We don't know yet—since it is in the balance,
Needing surgery on the obstructions,
        maybe impeachment,
Maybe to hear leisurely poems
     rather than war drums,
To see if we will recover
     from this national heart attack.

(On occasion when Disciples Peace Fellowship
commemorated September 11, 2001)

Counter Recruiting

The war making machine sneakily
     Spreads its tentacles into the schools
When a friendly recruiter leeringly
     Latches onto an innocent teenager.

Spieling out the schmaltz sales talk,
     "You will want the best life possible,
And we can start you on that today,"
The recruiter feeds blind propaganda.

Rescuing youth from militarism
     Requires a dialogue at the railroad,

"To stop, look and listen" for the options,
And refuse to support the killing machine.

*(On occasion when recruiting is two billion too much;
I'm wondering how to save our youth from militarism)*

Crying

The world has lost
its sense of humor,
by its sick sick addiction
to the instruments of war.
And no matter how many peace marches
Try to intervene and say, 'Insanity.'
The addiction drives itself to the bottom,
Before it will listen to a voice of reason.

War's gone wrong,
No more song,
No one is laughing,
And people keep dying,
We need change
Before we give up
Crying.

(On occasion when it's hard to endure the anguish of war)

Final Regrets

Poised to build a Bombplex,
When we might peer over the nuclear abyss,
And ask ourselves if it is worth the potential
For destruction and finality, for someone at least,
We would probably come to the edge later, with regrets.
We would ask if we could learn anything

About heeding Eisenhower's warning that
Every gun that is made signifies
    a theft from the poor,
and his conclusion that this is not
    a healthy way of life–
      this military industrial complex—
    that drains our soul
    of joy and life.

Our future on this planet
Could easily be destroyed
    By irresponsible decisions,
   Short sighted by economic interests,
   And moral bankruptcy,
   And fear of the phantom enemy.
That today many of us are motivated,
   Not by force, but rather by courage of convictions,
   That we are placed here to unite
    rather than divide,
    to make things better than
    to spend a lot of money to keep
    nations fearful.

The "Build up of arms" used to be called M.A.D.
   —Mutually Assured Destruction—
Which on the face of it is an insane idea,
    That could destroy the whole world,
And so what we are asking is a moral turn-around,
That could reverse a pro-war mentality,
    Which of course is the easy way out—
      And know that the real, genuine work
Requires peacemaking, not by force,
    but by nurturing communities
    and communicating through conflicts
    and not coming to the nuclear edge
      with final regrets.

(On the occasion of Bendix public hearing, May 27, 2007)

Imagine! Peace!

Imagine a day when the Department of Defense
No longer vacuums up all the money
    That could be traded to care for people,
. . . When corporations like the Military Industrial Complex
No longer sneak behind the right to privacy
And will examine the unethical practice of building weapons
That lead to death and destruction of civilians,
. . . When workers are concerned about building up
    Rather than tearing down the new creation,
Preventing global warming rather than scorching the earth,
. . . When policy makers begin to listen to peacemakers
Rather than trying to use force to outmaneuver them.
Imagine such a day!
    When we Imagine!Peace!

(On occasion in 2008 when peacemakers were trying to stop plans for a nuclear facility and we were appealing to the U.S. General Service Administrator)

Live Meditation

Sometimes resolving the tensions
Of peacemaking takes me into
    The present moment
Which nurtures the inner being,
    And gives a quiet energy of peace,
But changing the injustices
Means standing in the present
    And getting in the way
Of the money and the controllers
Of fear and the future,
    And so we have to let go
    And be true to our own self,
No matter the threats,
And how hard we beat up ourselves,

If we will be true to ourselves,
We will have a chance to live.

(On an occasion when a Sabbath moment brings a peace perspective)

Meanwhile, a War

A war is going on,
    And we pretend.
Maybe our trivialities
    Make lives end.

The aggression needs to stop
    Assuming we have the only right
To do whatever we want, whenever,
    While others shudder with fright.

A war is going on,
    And we pretend.
While powerless victims
    Just wish it would end.

(On occasion of reflecting what is normal, war or peace)

Obsession with Violence

How would we begin to transform a culture
That is tantalized by guns, spies, and war games?
When the downward spiral toward death is provocative
And we avoid a more humane treatment of others.

How do you address the fascination with war?
And stop stealing other resources like oil and land.
Or how about eliminating unfair capital punishment,
Maybe finding alternatives in the way we raise children.

Violence everywhere! Too bad it becomes the standard,
When what we need is to make non-violence normal,
Discovering that we not only hurt less people,
But we find peacemaking healthy to all living things.

*(On occasion in 2009 when American Friends Service Committee wonders how
the peacemaking movement breaks through the longevity of war)*

Of War and Peace

Whenever I hear the word "fascism"
    I cringe, because it represents
Such a black mark on public decency,
    Squelching the right to be free.

    You say that you are already free,
    That is, until you try to be different
And raise questions that go against
    The prevailing point of view.

Most people hear the word "peace"
    And they cringe over its softness,
Because it would ask us to be opposite
    Of our brutish, football mentality.

*(On occasion of facing the peace dilemma
when football and fascism present a contradiction)*

Pushing Pushiness

Push. Push. Push. Our nation snarls
    And others growl, some cower,
While we smugly savor our illusions
    Comforted by our majestic power.

Hypocrisy covers a nation's soul
    Until demands are like crying wolf,

As ineffective as catching Osama,
    Or curtailing Castro under our roof.

America is not the only game in town
    And the sooner we let the world be
And quit rattling our swords and teeth,
    More love, less fear for you and me.

(On occasion in realizing that people alligators
make meals out of the sensitive and soft spoken)

Quest for Peace

This quest for peace, fragile and illusive,
    Fights bombastic, strident voices, craving
To get there by force, brutally abusive,
    Completely dominating and enslaving.

War shows up in the gaps of life,
    Basically because of pressures
When we seek energy from strife
    And try to steal other treasures.

Peace comes to our sister and brother,
    After resolving the gaps of violence,
Not subjugating but respecting the other
    Even walking away from any offense.

Peace calls us onto the other side,
    To learn something about the quest,
Not violence and killing and pride,
    But finding ourselves in Sabbath rest.

(On occasion of seeking the best peace)

Sabbatizing Peace

Shalom, Salaam, Peace,
Sabbatize us in your vision of peace,
Where we no longer justify our conflicts,
Torture, or any meanness to our enemies—
Instead,
Let us turn from violence, fear,
And resolve war with the energy of love,
By courage within to work for justice,
And building up a new and humane creation.

(On occasion of making a good statement on peace)

Sacred C. O. W.

We are holding up these signs
About the "Cost Of War," asserting
That, one day of the Iraq war
Equals 720 million dollars,
Or 95,364 head start places for children
Or 84 new elementary schools
Or 6,482 families with homes,
When someone went by, shunning the flyer
Saying, "That is the price of freedom."

Really! Lost lives, lost dollars, lost morality,
When we could end the Iraq war,
Bring the troops home, unoccupy Iraq,
And redirect tax dollars to meet human need,
Money, Defense Contractors, Blackwater—
Forced freedom has a hollow ring to it.

Isn't it about time to kill the sacred cow?

(On occasion of questioning how patriotism gets in the way of clear thinking)

Souled Out

A nation that is comfortable
   With huge missiles and big guns
   And power and money and force
As a means of protection
     While calling for patriotism
Will soon find that it has sold out
   To values that cheapen
      the human spirit
And seduced some into the macho military
To quicken a day of destruction
When we can no longer put out
   the global oily fire
Because we have lost the opportunity
   To do something about our demise,
As we go the way of the dinosaur,
Or become like trance-like dopes
   Monkeying around
   With sticks of dynamite?
Perhaps, we can search for illusive hope
   By hiding the matches
   Or go one more day to pray for peace
   Or do some constructive act for the poor
   Or expose the government's deceit
   Or take time to transform our soul.

(On occasion of asking what we sell our soul for)

Speaking Out So Silently

We go along, go along, sometimes
   Speaking out not so silently,
  Even though we are afraid,
Afraid to admit that we don't
  Know what we are doing.

How we got to be a nuclear giant
    Turns out to be the same reasons
    That we became bullies of the world—
Some did it while nobody was looking.

Now, we seem to be ethical infants,
    Helpless to the consequences of
    Building up weapons of massive death,
Because bigger looks more powerful so
    We risk extermination of the human family.

The noise of war squashes voices of dissent,
    While Wall St. rings in the decline and fall
    Of the empire, addicted to its oily weapons,
      As the rich design schemes of profit,
      And the poor become poorer—
      Starving for hope, because
The world knows more about pain than living.

Still, we can not silence this yearning for peace.

(On occasion of 2008 public hearing at Kansas City's City Hall about land approval for building components for nuclear weapons)

Still Voices of Hidden Heroes

From the first day of shock and awe,
    To the 4,000 soldier deaths
    And the start of the sixth year,
In between—we untangle lies about war.

And minority voices are suppressed
    From raising searching questions
And pioneering through the quagmire
    Of mayhem and slaughter of innocent lives.

Power—all about dominance

To mimic the talking points
Of cardboard leaders who promote war,
Controlling, pushing and cajoling us
To wallow in their cesspool of deceit.

Yet brave peacemakers pled, "Stop this insanity."
And today we are here to thank 23 Senators,
    Immortals who voted against this immoral war,
    Which disdains whatever it touches.

For anyone who has spoken against
    The prevailing culture, controlled by war
And patriotic zeal and military might,
      We join them today and proclaim,
        "You are the real heroes!
    With honest voices that really count."

And a tear falls on the map of a country spiraling
    Out of control and dampens the pages of deceit,
So that we want to turn to the next chapter
    And read about real heroes who stood for peace.

From the first day of a dead soldier,
    To the last silent day of this war,
In between—we still yearn and act for peace.

(On the occasion of marking 4,000 soldier deaths
with a candlelight vigil at J.C. Nichols Fountain, Kansas City)

Stop the Pounding

Kaboom! Kaboom! The cadence of war.
Pounding, Obnoxious, Threatening Stomps.
    Marching over our sense of what's right
And making all of us insensitive monsters.

Voices in the wilderness cry out for peace,
But the pounding forces us to remain numb
And we can not think or do the right thing,
So we only go along with the brutality.

Why? Pounding in our heads. Why?
Do the rest have to suffer for the thieves,
   Who steal our souls and occupy our space,
Building walls instead of being fair to others.

Please, please, stop the pounding in my ears
   Of religions with the easy, hard answers,
   Or shoppers who walk around in a trance,
Even supporters of troops who condone war.

            (On occasion of rebelling against the noise of war)

The Hub

Today we are guests of honor
     invited as we are
        on the fourth anniversary
        of the Iraq war
to gather at the hub to say bullets fail—
when will peace prevail . . .

In a precarious time, behind a barricade
     are the police protectors for people
     and the plant, mostly the plant,
where non-union workers do the bidding
     of the war machine, pounding, cranking,
       each day and night, never stopping, ever more,
       six million bullets, polished and flashy,
some winding up in holsters of our protectors,
     who peek out with bullet proof eyes,
     immune to the soft ways, not crossing over,
     but wondering why we are here.

Because they also like to call themselves
            peacemakers,
but of course, with force, or do they routinely say
            peace with strength . . .
but that's the dark duty of their job,
        across the invisible impasse of Lake City.

If only we on this side of Hwy 7 would go away,
        Leave the bullets and secrets to their domain,
        And if only they could go home and prop themselves
            Up in an easy chair,
            Pop a cold one and forget . . .
That these cash bullets travel unconsciously into the weapons
        of a far away war in Iraq and Afghanistan,
        of genocide in Uganda, Rwanda, Sudan,
        of vulgar violence in every media of our being,
        of the haunting cries of mothers
            hovered over butchered bodies
                in streams of blood.
They may love the mantra. It's a good thing that people need bullets,
        to survive . . . or is it to mourn the world's future?

We look out at the hub
        and wonder how crazy life has become,
        and if we were driving around this circle
        in our cars of mobility with painted placards
        of sanguine red, frost white and aqua blue signs
        as if we were on a merry-go-round,
            unable to get off,
        that's how it is—busy and dizzy,
        without direction, just circles.

But what if we breathed in the imagination of a poet
        using words, quicker than bullets, to touch the heart.
And turned this hub into a peace sanctuary,
And what if it appeared from above like an axle
        centered in the middle, rising up to become an
antenna, beaming out waves of energy, for a healing peace,
        and what if we used a cosmic vacuum
            to channel all the bullets

and all the history of violence,
   plunging them down a drain,
so that we only saw a crater seared and stamped in the earth,
   a memorial of a peace symbol,
      to remind us to take
the road of the peacemaker
   and remember a communion
      where both sides understand each other
   and forget the bullets.

We would have to shiver a little,
   As the maples show the fragile red buds on the tips of limbs,
      The grass turns from a scruffy brown to a sleek green,
         when springtime is start up time,
            And a renewal for PEACE,

(On the occasion of the first peace rally at Lake City Army Ammunition Plant,
planned by Kansas City Iraq Task Force, on May 18, 2007)

The Leaves of Peace

It was brighter than most days during this time of year,
The yellow and red and brown leaves fell helplessly still,
As rescue rakes waited to pile high, Guernica's leaves,
Sweeping the trees bare and naked, unadorned and humbled.

Peaceful, isn't it? But unresolved in other parts of the world.
Or unresolved in the depths of the soul wherein lies war,
Hiding only a false peace, where it seems quiet, outwardly,
Maintained by a command of fear, suppression and force.

I suppose there are two kinds of peace, when one would do—
I'll take the one that resolves issues, listens to the other side,
Lets up on the control and assigns less moral and ingenuous blame.
Perhaps I would desire to be a leaf fluttering to my sacred ground?

(An autumn occasion for a deeper definition of peace)

The Memorial Day Wall

We come to this Viet Nam wall
knowing that there are immense parallels
to the current war that is taking so many lives
and in the "then and now"
we have a hard time justifying
wars built on lies and deceit.

But this will be our personal "wailing wall,"
To remember those innocents who died
    For purposes of their beliefs
    And for reasons we cannot know.
To reflect on our connection to the human family,
    Whereas someone suffers, we all suffer,
    When someone hurts from the other side,
      We all hurt and cry for their loss,
    Because we are world citizens pleading
      for a peaceful humanity.

We are here today to remember the dead
    And support the living,
That to remember is to have someone count,
    And that is all that we want anyway,
To be significant for someone and for something,
And hopefully it will be for the courage of our
    Convictions, that peace and justice
    Are goals worthy of our significance,
    No matter if we have to march
Against the popular or unpopular frenzy of war.

We are here to place down a flower,
    since we desire beauty, in spite of
the ugliness of war, the resistance to progress,
    That those who go before us,
      Have not died in vain,
      But are a witness and light for our path.

And so we come to this Viet Nam Wall,
>   To remember that we have much work to do,
>   Not to repeat every season of history,
>   Because we can resist the glorification of war,
And be about the business of peacemaking.

(On occasion for a 2007 Memorial Day Rally at the Wall in which Viet Nam Veterans confronted a large group of protesters of the Iraq war)

The Promise of War

Here come the spiffy recruiters
Promising adventure and travel,
Excitement and education,
>   Leading you off to war.

No big deal, they say,
You can be a hero,
A fighter for freedom,
>   Leading you off to kill.
Here come the spiffy recruiters,
Beware, you might ask,
>   What do I sell my soul to?
And is this war worth the risk?

Here comes the spiffy recruiters,
I think not—the price is too high,
For innocent victims on both sides.
>   We should study war no more.

(On occasion of seeing recruiters in the High School)

The Secrecy of War

When will we ever learn, lamented over again
    That the reasons for war remain secret,
Hidden behind the brainwashing of a nation,
    Entangled in a quagmire of untruths.

Some patriots say that we need a surge,
    Not another Viet Nam, but to win—what?
When the perception of more occupiers
    Can only inflame reaction and rage.

Others will say that we have got to keep
    The war over there, not in our streets,
But we will see the damage come home
    As soldiers return carrying dark violence.

Some veterans assert that the war must continue
    So that the dead will not have died in vain,
But the secret will whisper that we have been
    Fighting an unnecessary and meaningless war.

The supporters will claim that we are sacrificing
    For freedom and democracy and American pride
When the real secret has more to do with exacting
    Oil control, regime change and empire domination.

    Other patriots would stridently have us believe
    That our presence is stabilizing the Middle East
When actually the country is in worse shape
    And our visibility reminds them of Israeli apartheid.

So many disconnected voices hiding so many secrets,
    Manipulated to believe in a huge defense budget,
When programs for the poor are callously neglected,
    And we wind up selling our soul to greed and death.

The greed for more money feeds the war monster,

Which results in more fear, more indebtedness,
More distrust, more distractions from real life issues—
Please—no more secrets—we want peace!

(On occasion when justifying war is so secret)

The Surge of Walnuts

If only a walnut from my leaning tree
    Could hit a candidate in the head,
Maybe he wouldn't continue the myth
    That the surge in Iraq has worked.

Groan. Sure the casualties declined,
But the real reason has more to do
    With military pay to the insurgents,
    The pull back of Muqtad al-Sadr,
    The concrete walls that separate,
    The ethnic Sunni repression,
Which led some to false impressions
    That America has a small victory.
Groan. All we have is hypocrisy
    And a WalNut in the Whitehouse.

If only we could get hit in the head
    And surge up a better perspective that
    We are occupiers and war bullies and
    Distributors of anti-Americanism.
Groan. The walnuts cover my yard
    As many as bombs on the truth.

(On occasion during the 2008 Bush era when decrying more troops in Iraq)

Too Much 911

Questions Questions Questions
    A conspiracy of why's on 9/11
An explosion below?
A missile into the Pentagon?
A cover up by the government.
    Well, that's why, they lie.

Maybe we should call 911.

(On occasion when answers are inadequate)

Under the Mushroom Cloud

I guess common sense
    Would be too common,
Not exotic enough to wonder
    Why we keep building bombs
For bigger and better genocide,
    Just in case we need to use them,
So that we won't use them like
    We did on Hiroshima and Nagasaki,
But that's some plus three score years later,
    Where we haven't even had a nuclear
Accident, like in Dr. Strangelove, lucky us!

So we have wars,
    So we melt the polar caps,
        So we spend half on the military
            So we flirt with radiation,
And don't think anything about it,
    Paralyzed, inertia, never change our course,

And if we could we would,
    But getting 51% to change their thinking
Would be difficult, but not impossible,
    If we could start with 5% awakened activists.

I wonder if we have become too smart
    In the wrong things, but not smart enough
To use our common sense—
    As we wonder what else could go wrong,
    Under the cloudy corporate mushroom cloud

Where's the problem . . .
        weapons or life.

(On occasion of wondering about the 64th year since Nagasaki
by gonging a cymbal when the string broke and the cymbal fell into the lake of
Loose Park and we laughed at what else could go wrong)

Unraveling

Terrorists attacked on 911,
    And the empire shook in fear,
Looking down a painfully perilous path,
Relying on preemptive military force,
    And favoring large corporations
To create more profits and more empire,
So that power and privilege would rule.
The shock of two towers falling,
Set up a precarious alliance, whereby
    The government adopted the mantra
Of privatization through corporations
And now workers served an allied institution,
    Or else they might be fired,
And thus the life energy of a nation was drained
    Into an obsessive pursuit of money
And shifted out of the sensitive care for others,
    Disregarding the nurture of people
By eroding a caring community—Mindless,
Most people were numbed into slavery.

Fighting terrorism became a convenient way
For the controllers of power to hold onto power
And eliminate the liberties of individuals,
So that the control of others created the cement
        Of a rigid Orwellian 1984 society,
Oh, by another number 911, revisited and painfully real,
        Where only the brave few were resisting,
And the cautious majority conveniently fell into place,
        And the war dragged on and
            on and on by its own inertia.

While most went shopping, finding distractions,
Dumbing themselves into entertainment receptacles,
        Perched in front of the TV sports channel,
Moving a bit with a big play but meaninglessly,
And stepping outside to watch the latest development
        On a golf course or a shopping center,
As the bulldozers scalp the earth into huge mounds
And scrape the life-giving trees into a far corner to burn,
        And the Walmarts of the world stubbornly go up
And later put up "out of business" signs with all the other competitors,
Leaving a shell of dilapidated towns and out of work signs,
        And this notion of progress keeps destroying the earth,
Setting up global warming disasters, some close to home,
Causing the growth of a humongous trade deficit,
And hemorrhaging people to spend beyond their means,
        So the pain is deep, shocking, torturous, debt stained,
Thus unraveling the hypocrisy of a once good way of life.

Nevertheless we must point to a different path,
        For the great unraveling must move beyond
        All the missteps of control and Empire,
Because we are sick of slavery and servitude,
And tired of intolerable crimes on humanity,
Since we would just like to die to empire,
Halt its efforts to maintain domination,
And the destructive consequences of competition,
And turn around a bend in a different direction

From domination to community,
From me-ness to we-ness.

We stand at a stage in history,
With a choice of domination
Or partnership in community,
By reattaching ourselves to this earth,
    And caring about those values
    That help our species to survive.

This is a defining moment but we have to change,
And break the silence and snap out of the despair.
    And reach into the poetry of our hearts,
      To liberate our higher consciousness,
And tell a different story,
    From the old stories of dominance,
    And the brainwashing of democracy,
    And stealing land from Indians,
    And resisting the voice of women,
    And splitting immigrant families apart,
    And ignoring the concerns of minorities.
Yes, we have to change and feel the national pain
And take democracy to a new place…
Displacing the stories of dominant empire
    Into a new community of rebirth and celebration.

Changing the world takes each person involved
    From militarism to nurturing communities,
    From squandered moments to vibrant movements,
    From looking to the outside to the mysteries within,
As each unravels the pain and we move forward in peace.

    (On occasion when the empire bottoms out and looks up, if . . .)

Waiting to be Dead

So much of life is like this,
Waiting to be dead,
    So we play with
    Bullets instead,
Some just wait
And only live late.

    (On occasion when getting older is not the answer to the meaning of life)

War and Wrestling

At times, War looks like Pro Wrestling,
    To wit, entertainment, built on a pompous lie.
Posturing brutality and flexing muscles,
    Except in the display of war, too many die.

    (On occasion when war is not entertainment)

War Boomeranged

Too many cheerleaders
    Supporting our troops
Are walking in a fog,
By repeating the mistakes
    That glorify war.

War creeps on the shore
    In the pain of Veterans,
Suffering 18 suicides a day,
And 200,000 homeless,
And too much Post Trauma
    Frustratingly crying out
Not to recycle war at home.

War is not intelligent,
        And tramples on our soul,
So we need wise leadership
        To switch our resolve
And abolish militarism
        That destroys our sanity,
Returning peace back home,
        Calming the war within.

(On occasion when war is an outreach of ourselves)

Waste Management Plant

Winding up at a Casino,
        With flashing lights and
        An hypnotic dull melody
        muddling the noisy buzz
        with an occasional bell ringing,
A row of persons perch themselves
        on stools before video slots,
        with blank stares,
        and empty expressions,
        and dead pan eyes.
Ready to be wasted.
Amused, a war is going on,
        And someone is wasted daily,
Here nobody notices,
        And eyes are glazed
        Like doughnuts
        with holes transfixed.
Waiting for the jackpot,
        With one more killed
        And another killing time,
Ready to be wasted.

*(On occasion of visiting a casino where loads of money
are put into the slots for entertainment)*

What For?

I wonder what this war is for,
> To fight, to die, to ask why?
Is it to pit the rich against the poor.
> Or maybe, to steal for some big lie.

Enough of the idolatry of war,
> Where deception is the goal,
If it kills and maims!—no more—
> This draining of the human soul.

(On occasion of still wondering why war)

When Will Any Bully Listen?

Bullies just seem to like a good fight,
> And they don't care if someone gets hurt,
Or that nobody likes them or reacts to them,
> Because then you would have to feel pain.

They love hiding behind their illusion of security,
Wrapping in fear what they don't want to reveal,
> That they are scared too,
Making up a government that will not listen,
And attacking others who are different than them.

Our nation blew up El Qaeda the Boogey man
Bigger than life because of the Iraq war,
And our stance with military support of Israel,
But allowed the escape of spiritual guru Osama Bin Laden,
Reacting to destroy the moral center of America's hubris,
> Teaching a lesson we will never forget,
Except we never received the lesson.

The West has humiliated Muslims
And caused a great deal of resentment,
    And because we have not listened,
And not even treated the rich with respect,
Many turned to religion to die as a martyr.

The myopia of American foreign policy
Frustrates the Muslim world with Iraq occupation,
Because we can not let go of our control, and oil, and . . .
    When will we learn a different lesson, that we are
Not safer by bullying or expanding an empire,
    When will the bullies ever learn?
Or, not even that, just stop trying to interfere
By thinking we are doing it for their own good.

(On occasion of confronting the bullies)

PART TWO

Worker Justice

Respect the Dignity of the Worker

What does the Lord require of you,
but to do justice, to love kindness
and walk humbly with your God.

MICAH 6:8

Compassionate Work

Labor and religion
Seeking justice for all,
Working together for a fair deal
   among the marginalized,
   the minimal wage earner,
   minorities,
   and immigrants.

A coalition advocating
     Justice for the poor,
  Dignity of personhood,
And standing with the poor,
    and the oppressed,
    and the left-out,
    and the dispossessed—
    anyone dehumanized.
This should be what we call
    Church and Christ's work.
Using the energy
   of compassionate work,
      to better the world.

(On occasion when thinking about Interfaith Worker Justice goals)

From Work to Leisure

People are still striving to outdo each other,
Looking for significance in their work,
Trying to say, "I amount to something."
Because of what I have and what I do.

What if we end up at the other end of life
And discover that we spent a lot of time on triviality
And that our energies were not on the big issues,
That our philosophies were selfish and arrested.

That we never faced into the pain of knowing
Who we belonged to and what it is that is really significant,
     Like peace and justice and ecology,
And that at the other end of life—
               authenticity.

What if we could use the road blocks of our upward climb,
To realize that the work of peace is an authentic expression
     Of our leisure,
          simply being who we are,
Without having to be noticed or manipulative.

     We come to a point in life
When we ask what our work has produced,
And how will we cope with leisure, hopefully,
When irrelevant is
     the question of retirement.

(On occasion when facing retirement)

Just a Little Lie

One lie after another,
     Doesn't matter the next time
Just a way of life
     And if the people forget
And want to believe . . . then
     It's a new moment, a new lie,
That's the way it's done
     When you're hiding greed,
Except there's a problem:
     History may not bury the lie.

(On occasion when the media needs to uncover the truth)

Justice for Janitors

Today we celebrate the work of janitors,
Working behind the scenes to make lives
Feel better about a cleaner environment,
And bring vision to that which hope strives.

When managers underestimate the dignity
Of their workers, debasing their self-esteem,
By taking advantage of a greedy situation,
They rob all of us who aspire to a better dream.

Let us look to those who have courage
To yearn for justice and take up the cause
With the poor, whose labor sustains our lives
And fixes our brokenness—making us pause.

Let us not forget the plight of our janitors,
Who clean our buildings and save us each hour,

Since we are taking care of God's creation,
        Lifting our spirits,
                whom janitors can empower.

(On occasion at a rally standing for better wages for janitors)

Listen to the Snowflakes

Snow flakes are falling outside,
        But inside Honeywell it's a job
For a giant military contract,
        Oblivious to whom they rob.

Just a job to produce weapons,
        And contaminate the green earth,
But nobody really wants to know,
        About the values of our nation's birth.

One wonders what's at stake here,
    As if the desire for nuclear security
Takes precedence over authentic life,
    As we contaminate our ethical purity.

We should cease our stockpiling of fear,
    And ask if our jobs really help our survival,
Or contribute to the end of humanity—
    Quietly snowflakes wipe away any ghostly rival.

(On occasion of Second Public Hearing on 1/9/08 to stop the Bendix plant)

Looking for Work

You don't want to do work you hate,
So you look for work that is constructive
Or produces a product improving human kind—
Not only to pay bills but work you believe in.

BS work doesn't allow you to be yourself—
    It's for show, for prestige, for money,
Or we can disassociate ourselves from the task
    And perform even torture if necessary.

Look at the guards on death row,
    They are assigned a job to kill someone
But since they have only a role to fill,
They can absolve themselves from responsibility.

Too many are looking for work,
    Taking jobs just to survive and hold on,
Too many feel like they have no choice,
    Hoping someday to find the work of dreams.

(On occasion of realizing that only self-employment fits)

Out of Work

The fish are gulping for air
　　　Underneath the icy sheet,
Half-dead, half frozen,
　　　They must be unemployed.

(On occasion when realizing that life can be hard)

Over Worked

So much of it is meant to make
　　　One feel insignificant—
The pile of papers alarmingly high,
　　The complexity of new language,
　　　The volume of overchoice
So the government doesn't work
Yet the military thinks it does,
　　Til it gets caught killing life,
　　While the body piles up stress,
　　　And people feel stretched,
Til they just give up their projects
　　And go out with the sunset.

(On occasion when jobs disappear and stress takes over)

Soft Welcomed Snow

The light snow lays down a blanket
　　　As workers snuggle by the fireplace
And forget their struggles to survive,
　　　While pausing to enjoy a slower pace.

Pesky snow offers a break in the action,
    Ceasing competition between his and hers,
When what we need is to huddle close
    And share more about becoming partners.
    The world is heavy with cruel domination
    And we forget to show others a kind way,
Fewer barbs. Softer nurturing responses,
    Gently like a surprising sneaky snow day.

(On a January occasion when things pause)

Sounds from the Basement

Joking about losing a job is cruel,
Cutting to the heart of our whole being,
Taking away our dignity to be significant,
Our link with family and helping others.

The lowest wages for the most work,
Doing jobs that nobody else will do,
Treats the worker less than human,
Muffling out voices by a firing squad.

The threat disrupts our tie with tomorrow,
Shattering hope, shaking us with fear,
A technique used by the employer
To force compliance of the worker.

One voice complaining can sound another,
Until many voices rise from the basement,
Overtaking the stuffed ears on the top floor,
For if work needs a foundation, the top listens.

(On occasion when firing is not a nonchalant event to keep obedient workers)

Tearing Down or Building up the Wall?

Our tears flow for workers around the world
      Who sweat away to make America comfortable.
For the wall will crumble under the abuse of money
      Piled high on the backs of slave labor.
We must raise up a sacred foolishness
      That would question the status quo of corporate greed
And rebuild a Wal that puts people before profits,
      that pays a fair share for the public good.
Will we continue to build walls for the wealthy
      and keep tearing down walls that protect the poor?
Might all of us pause and dread the day that a wall
      could ever insulate us from tears of compassion!

*(On occasion for a poetry slam when Walmart
was setting the standard for retail work)*

The Tale of Two Tyrannies

Walmart—it used to be the best of times
      when we had fuzzy feelings about Sam Walton
and his long ago story about taking care of employees,
      but now suddenly it seems like the worst of times.

Suddenly we sense that a war has turned on us
      And what was "Made in America"
has moved overseas to bring in more profits,
      and compassionate care for employees
            seems tossed on the side of the road,
            littering the street with confused,
crumpled up unemployables.

We could draw upon poetic imagery to visualize a box
        contained within a box, looking alike on the outside,
        except the boxes are huge,
            a nation contained within a nation,
            with secret compartments for union busters

and young, tense managers,
ready to strike back at bristly critics,
        who just might expose truth to national power,
                where one runs weapon sales
                and the other shopping sales,
        but each is on the prowl for profits,
                the one is empowering China
                and the other is beholding to China,
                and both never question that they may be
                foretelling their own collapse.

They'll say, "Our empires didn't see it coming."

The two nations stay alive by demanding obedience
        from citizens and the work force,
        and so they perpetuate a bleak consciousness
where nothing really changes,
        except the rich get richer, and the poor
                —you know, the down-forgotten—
where universal health care
        and freedom to organize
                and respect of employees
are far away from a vision of an American dream
that only gets talked about.

Someday when the tale of two tyrannies,
Will no longer have to be told,
And can be replaced by legends in which
America and Walmart are able to move
                to a more generous tomorrow,
we can cease beating the rest of the world up
                with guns and greed. If only.

Today we worry about ports of entry,
Because two tyrannies stir up the world
        into a hostile hornet's nest
And fear has built "Walls of Mourning" to keep people apart,
When what we really need are exports of

giving authentic kindness,
> not stealing another's natural resource,
> disturbingly repeated from past conquests
> for land, gold, diamonds or oil.

Someday it starts out one at a time,
> When we can say "No,
I can't take it any longer," this system that
can reward the rich and step on the poor
and turn us all into objects and commodities,
> not even good enough to be recycled.
Then, then we join three or more to create
> communities of vigilant resistance.

We wait for a steady breeze
> to stir our hard hearts
> And the last pin oak leaf to somersault
> across our fields of imagination,
> And a refreshing rain
> to soak deep into the ground of our being
> to turn the disheveled, crusty brown into a grinning, grassy green.
For today, the start-up time of spring is everywhere,
> As it should be,
> Only now we wait for companies like Walmart
to grow,
> mature,
be transformed
> into a spring time
> of nurturing its best resource and product –
> which would be people, sensitive to workers,
> justice for the PEOPLE.

> *(On 2007 occasion at Blue Ridge Mall over Walmart's intent*
> *to inspect only 5% of ports)*

The Truck Driver Nowhere

What is so disturbing about
the retired truck driver asserting
I'm not going to vote in November
Because I'm retired and don't care,
After rattling off a progeny of kids
And he doesn't care what happens,
Proudly driving his truck
    nowhere,
       He failed to stop and load his Semi
With a new set of values—so he drove
Into the dark night with his empty truck,
Because he failed to turn on
    his lights.

(On occasion of hearing apathy before the 2008 election)

The Wall of No Sides

Fear builds a wall with two sides,
    Tall with suspicion and hatred,
Fooled by a false assumption
    That the other side is really different.

The rage inside piles up because of check points,
    And waiting and seething and feeling the red tape,
That nobody cares if you are treated decently,
    Like you will never ever have the right credentials.

Once a young woman stood between home and bulldozer
    To die for a principle that stealing is unacceptable
For lives and homes and a right to the neighborhood.
    She faced a force that could not destroy human dignity.

The Wall—grey-faced, hardened, imposing—divides,

Making one side feel superior to the other,
Which sets up one of the strange hoaxes of humanity,
    Til those aware can look pass the walls of no sides.

Who will confront the powerful who put up walls of deceit,
    By seeking to do justice and love kindness and forgiveness,
Lamenting every myopic, false wall of apartheid?
    Come now, the next creative courageous peacemakers!

(On occasion in remembering Rachel Corrie killed in April
by standing between a bulldozer and a Palestinian home
and her attempt to bring down walls of apartheid)

The Wisdom of a Janitor

    Janitors are near the heart of God
Since they are humble servants to others,
    Taking care of buildings and people,
Stopping along the way to work and listen.

    Listening between the rhythmic sweeping
Swish, swish heartbeat of God's activity
Helps us realize that the energy of cleaning
    Contributes to a divine work of love.

(On occasion of the March 27, 2009
loss of Larry Gehlken, his friendship and his rapport)

To Be Significant

To be significant
    Or not to be
Teases the question
    Want to live or die?

But to live is
> To know and to do
To take up vocation
> To align it with awareness.

To know and not to do
> Is not to live.
Not to know and to do
> Is meaninglessness.

Therefore to know and to do
> Is to *live* authentically.
Show me Peace Justice and Ecology
And life will be *significantly* yours.

(On occasion of wondering how our work makes a difference)

Ugly Negotiations

They came, tight-lipped,
> Distantly lined up
>> Like scare crows
>> On a telephone wire,
> Hiding little secrets
>> Behind closed doors,
>> Away from public scrutiny,
To do their dirty deeds,
> Gaining an advantage,
>> Of more tricks than treats,
While keeping the Union waiting,
> And waiting, and trying
>> To observe some bleeding,
>> Or find a better deal, because
To be a manager can be ugly.

*(On occasion when management tried to outmaneuver
nurse negotiators to thwart the union)*

Part Three

Immigration

Welcome the Stranger

God shows no partiality.

Heb 5:13

Crossings

We clasp the hand of those who follow a vision,
And carry the hearts of those who face unbelievable strife.
As we, fellow immigrants, seek a sanctuary of freedom,
For those crossing all personal borders for a better life.

(On occasion when Immigration Justice Advocacy Movement seeks out a vision)

Denials of Racism

The public chorus sings,
  "I'm no racist,"
Or at least
  I don't feel like one,
Yet I do things that promote racism.

  Here's the big deal,
Maybe you don't
  appear to be racist,
Since you can joke with people of color,
Yet you can't really feel empathy
For the pain of marginalized groups,
  Who are daily dehumanized
  By power and the privileged.

"I'm no racist," denies
Institutional racism
  that puts people down
  and targets persons by color,
  and because one can't recognize

or one pridefully dismisses
        the voice of minorities, or even
    ignores a language of respect,
Indeed you may be racist
            And not even know it.
Denying how others perceive you
        Doesn't eliminate racism,
But humbly recognizing that
One is not superior to another—
        It's a healthy good first step
In joining the human race
        Without being attached
            to an "ism."

(On occasion when racism seems tiresome)

Faceless

Show the face of America
        And of what do we see—
Blurred vision of faceless faces
        Of the tired and poor, no liberty.

Oh how can the tight faces
        Strike pain into the heart
Of the immigrant and show
        Intolerance to keep them apart,

Yet, this is the world we live in,
        Meanness, harm to others,
No flexibility to look the other way,
        Only to deport our faceless brothers.

(On occasion of realizing that a number of people
would not put their photo in Facebook)

Go into Sanctuary

I. C. E. Enforcers come before you awake,
Hand cuffing suspected illegal immigrants
Tearing families apart, emotionally separated,
Yearning to once again touch what is missing.

All of us make a journey, long and hard,
With many personal borders to cross,
But in a land of immigrants it is painful
To stand by and watch victims of unjust laws.

The law seems to be brittle and harsh,
When it refuses to look at circumstances,
And only pays attention to the proper papers,
While ignoring a higher law of hospitality.

Come . . . go . . . into peaceful sanctuary.
Where we can find Sabbath rest and safety,
From the punitive, judgmental enforcers,
Who feel so righteous in following the law.

And so we have some broken laws to fix,
Not to take advantage of the poor and needy,
But to treat immigrants with the same justice
And compassion that God has shown to us.

*(On occasion when punitive laws hurt and must give way
to a humane and compassionate immigration policy)*

I. C. E. Breaker

Running from officials of I. C. E.
　　Who play the game of deportation
Leaves a chilling fear in the price
　　Of freedom to see one's destination.

Immigrants come and come and welcome
　　Waves of struggle seeking new opportunities,
Like anyone, everywhere, seeking home,
　　Free from racism and abusive impunities.

We need to hold a big Mardi Gras, unafraid,
　　Where everyone is invited to find love,
And the ice breaker would be a parade
　　Tossing candy, beads, and kisses above.

(On occasion when Immigration & Customs Enforcement rounded up and detained day workers, wishing for something less punitive)

Justice for All Immigrants

We are a nation of immigrants
Who come from as far as Mexico
　　　And Central America,
　　　Ireland, Sudan and Iraq,
Escaping from poverty and fear
　　　And war and suppression,
Leaving behind somebody
　　　In a former homeland.
We bring our language, pictures,
　　　Back packs, stories and hopes,
Having crossed desserts and steep hills
Hopped trains, befriended coyotes,
　　　Smugglers of desperate refugees.
Called illegals and undocumented terrorists,
We are rounded up at work, imprisoned
　　　And deported and we disappear
But we keep coming back to wash your dishes

In restaurants in Kansas City, or rebuild
The homes of New Orleans,
>Or pick apples in Yakima
>And put roofs on houses
>>In small towns and big cities.
Since we are your brothers and sisters,
>Children of our Creator.
Deserving respect, dignity and
>Recognition of our common humanity,
With the same opportunities for our families
Of equality, life, liberty
>And the pursuit of happiness.

(On occasion to send a clarion call to realize the dignity of other human beings)

Labeling

It is easy to label others,
Since putting people in boxes
Maintains a separateness
And keeps people from bothering us.

We do it with immigrants,
Undocumented workers,
>Economic refugees,
Like calling people names,
>Makes us feel superior,
>Fits out comfort zones
If we can keep people distant.

Name calling does hurt us
>As much as sticks and stones,
And may last longer to prevent
>Seeing all
>>as a child of God.

*(On occasion of Immigration Justice Advocacy Movement
thinking about a statement for changing us into a just world)*

Mile High Hope

Obama energizes the Democrats
Dreams the dream of M.L.K.
But why, why do some wrap the flag
Around "God Bless America."

The mantra creates a small America
That leans toward empire building
And all those greedy tendencies
That will pull America down.

If we were to be open to the dream,
We would be open to the immigrants,
No matter where they come from,
We would treat them with dignity.

The problem is that no matter how
You articulate the dream, some
Do not get it and never will, because
They stay safe in their small cage.

But the hope is that others will look
Beyond the cage and open up
To a bigger vision of world citizenship,
That's the growth of a real American.

(On August 28, 2008 occasion when Obama accepted
the Democratic nomination)

Only a Minuteman

We are tossed about like little leaves
In a wind storm looking for a place to hide
As the wind chimes sing a restless melody
And life rushes by ever so noisy and huffy.

Yet a quiet place resides hidden from view,
Where one feels a warm glow of victory,
Because one struggled so long with the pain
Of minority voices seeking to put hate behind.

The Minutemen came to the city, anger filled,
Spewing their intolerance like clanging trash cans,
Idolizing one of their own who defied wisdom
To join a vigilante group and see nothing wrong.

It didn't matter how it happen, just that it did,
When she resigned, the city, everybody won,
Including the mayor, Saul Alinsky, M.L.K., I.W.J.,
And the Latino community, all became one.

And life rushes by ever so noisy and huffy,
While most the time we barely cause a whimper
But every once in awhile we can taste victory
And smiling we feel attached to a strong oak tree.

(On occasion of January 29, 2008 when a rally was waged
against a Minutemen conference in Kansas City)

Overcoming Suspicions

Americans have immigration amnesia
　　And keep spouting the usual negativity
As if today's immigrants are so different,
　　Since each wave has faced discrimination
Before being welcomed and appreciated.

We need the variegated Obama revolution,
　　To wipe clean the slate of intolerance
And accept every person as a valuable

Contributor to our immense country
Rather than viewing them as terrorists.

(On occasion when we need to be tolerant of diversity)

Pea Soup

Two peas in a pod,
　　Exceptionalism and chosenness,
　　Empire and expansionism.
　　　　Second comings and Zionism,
　　　　Iraq and Gaza,
　　　　Militarism and settlements,
　　Native Americans and Palestinians,
　　United States and Israel,
Two peas in a pod,
　　A recipe for making split pea soup,
Not that everyone likes pea soup.

(On occasion of thinking that our liaisons might be a barrier)

Plight

The cries of a people go unheard,
　　　Just to get food and medical supplies
To the prisoners of the Gaza strip,
　　　Stripped of dignity and mobility.
Each side accusing the other of terrorism,
　　　　Except the unlucky mother with a child
　　　　Sucking her toe who stops breathing,
　　　One by one the killing raises the violence.

　　　Only the numbness stops the tears,
　　When we can not feel any more horror,

And those who go into their comfort zone,
    Shut out the horror, shut in a personal prison,
While the Palestinians turn into stone silence.

(On occasion of hearing George Galloway, Member of Parliament,
speak on July 2 in Kansas City at a "Viva Palestina" fundraiser
before taking a convoy into the Gaza Strip on July 10, 2009)

Puff Balls

Dandelions, everywhere, all over the lawn.
    Out of place, just a yellow weed,
Like all of us who don't fit trimmed lawns,
    Popping up where we don't belong,
Transformed into white puff balls
    Light, airy, and floating by the wind,
We are the seeds that offer beauty to children.

(On occasion of thinking how the variety of immigrants
adds beauty to an otherwise dull, predictable world)

Recklessness

Pushing and shoving humanity
    On the other side of a wall
Is hardly a good solution for
    Scapegoating the problems within.

For we have a war to fight
    And a bailout to pay for,
And a way of life to defend,
    Not living within our means.
All we have to do is
    Swipe the credit card,
And blame the immigrants—
    Away our troubles will go.

We are littering the landscape,
      With consumers in debt
And are being entertained,
By a country going down.

*(On occasion in September 2008 when the bailout was supposed to turn
the economy around but we had reason to be skeptical)*

Remembering Lazarus

Give me your culture of adventure,
      A country that respects freedom,
And democracy, that allows
          dissent
As a vigorous sign of patriotism, not fear
That one might not
      control the world
Or take away from other's resources.

Give me a country that treats immigrants
      As real persons
          who desire dignified work
That contribute to this culture of adventure,
Because there is a feeling for open borders,
A love to embrace
      others more than fences,
A welcome mat to the weary traveler.

*(On the occasion of an Immigration Justice Advocacy Movement meeting and
recalling the Statue of Liberty motto, the best of the American dream)*

"Give me your tired, your poor,
Your huddled masses yearning to breathe free,
The wretched refuse of your teeming shore,
Send these, the homeless, tempest-tossed, to me,
I will lift my lamp beside the golden door."
—*Emma Lazarus*

Shifting Shadows

So staying one step ahead of the authorities
    While looking behind at the snitchers
Who live by the letter of the law
    And make life miserable for others
Certainly is a poor way to look ahead
Through the shifting shadows
Of the sun streaking across the earth
    And warming the immigrant
        in all of us
But revealing the fear of some frightened
    refugees,
Hoping for a welcoming light of day.

(On occasion of the fugitive status of immigrants)

Shopping

Down the corridor of the mall
Strolled nonchalant walkers
    Swaying to the beat of aimless music
Stepping off into the oblivion of
        nowhere.
Completely removed from the sounds of war
Or the screams of suffering in Iraq or the memory
Of someone who is despised,
    tortured and crucified,
Left out, forgotten,
    where life counts less and less.

The answer my friends is to go shopping,
So we have been told, to pump up the economy,
Then we can afford
    more weapons to slaughter
    The innocent passers by who interfere

With our forward motion—the easy flow,
The tired gait, the dazed look of numbed people
Just walking like they were lost in a fog.

Out of mind, out of sight, goes the immigrant,
Exiled from the homeland,
        forced to be refugees
In a land that turns its head and avoids eye contact,
Using racist dispersions and handling out papers
For the law, for deportations, for messages
That say we don't want
        you, but be our slaves,

Pushed out, out of mind, get out of my way,
Says America, because I'm a different walker
And I have some serious buying to do, so
I must say Good bye to your pain, I'm too busy,
Shopping—forgetting the world's pain.

(On occasion of ignoring the world's problems)

Sojourners

Always people of faith on the move,
    Often moving through transitions
    Into new directions, new boundaries,
        New periods of history,
        From refugees to settlers,
            Even pilgrims passing
Through the valley of death,
God's people have always faced obstacles.

So all immigrants travel through the wilderness.
God's people offer hospitality,
    To the stranger, the refugee,
    Those who want to feed their family.
God's people are faithful to God's call

To those who are oppressed,
  To those suffering great hardships,
    To those forced from their homeland,
    To those who run into fear,
        Into the arms of a frightened people.

Let my immigrants go to find a better place.

We walk together with the sojourner
  And find our way together
    Around the table to become one
With every sojourner on a faith journey,
  Encouraged that we do not walk alone.

Let my people go!

(On occasion at the 2009 General Assembly of the Christian Church
(Disciples of Christ) of thinking about Biblical themes
that drive our faith to action for the immigrant)

Statue of Sand

Give me your tired and huddled poor,
    To let a stranger feel welcome in this land,
But too many hide behind the rigid law
    As if they are patriotic in dividing the sand.
Yet the sand blends together in many colors,
    And multi-cultural residents are here to stay,
Defying the dehumanizing and oppression
    Of undeveloped ideas looking for a better way.

Let's build a humane immigration policy,
    Not as fleeting as blowing sand, but reasonable,
Relying on a compassionate, warm welcome
    And respecting all persons who are teachable.

(On occasion for accepting different sands poured together)

Step Aside

The uniformed pot bellied officer
Behind the protected glass enclosure
     Asserted, with his bassoon voice,
 "Step Aside," meaning . . .
I'm about to ignore you,
I will not deal with you,
   You don't count,
      Rejected, excluded,
      Don't bother me.
      You're lost in blackness,
      Disappearing before my eyes,
Because I'm in a deportation mood,
And when I get like this,
     I'm coping with death
Of a human being sent far away,
You know, just doing my duty,
So don't make me think about suffering,
   Just, "Step Aside."

The refugee crosses space and time,
   Into an unwelcome no man's land,
Secretly avoiding legal authorities
   Until one day he is caught,
Entrapped by unknown suspicions,
Except he looks different
   And was singled out,
     Targeted to play the game
Of the illegal immigrant, innocently
Accused of fitting a phantom profile of the
     Terrorist,
So, another unfair judgment call,
Collateral damage of the government,
   Allowing another person to disappear,
     Until we can find out
     What has been lost—
     Perhaps the Statue of Liberty,
       Will have to "Step Aside."

(On occasion of seeing the movie "The Visitor")

The Mourning Walls Within

High are the walls that divide the land—
Walls that are signs that
      say, "No Trespassing"
To frighten away the no good, nobodies,
Who dare to come,
     step by step,
         to the other side.

The wall goes up steel by steel, slab by slab
      Jutting through the horizon
         between them and us
Slicing the common, invisible air we breathe,
Falsely assuming that the real estate
is ours.
One day the wall snakes around the settlements
Which assume to have the right to take away land
Like Palestinian "Indians" herded onto reservations
Surrounded by an expanse of grey,
speckled with tears.

In another way the wall goes up along the border,
Built to crack down on immigration—those needing work—
Which on a another day defined what it meant to be American,
But now the work we have is
     guards to protect the wall.

The wall that is closing in on us is a
     wall we put up inside,
A wall of fear and
     division between the rich and poor
For what we see from the outside causes concrete anger
That forces people to overcome violence with violence.

And the only way out is
        for leaders to tear down walls
Like the Berlin wall or the apartheid wall of South Africa,

When those in power come out from
behind their walls
And make the first move to remove any reason
for a wall.

(On occasion of remembering Berlin walls, Israeli walls, southern border walls)

The Sanctuary Railroad

We become the new underground railroad
To bring immigrants to a new sanctuary,
Wrapping them into the safety of churches,
Welcoming strangers with warm hospitality.

We must find the courage to be the new
John Browns who risked their lives
To free slaves from the task masters
And avoid the Quantrills of his time.

We are called into a new day and challenge
To build a bigger vision of tolerance
For the different, oppressed and forgotten
To respect the human dignity of all.
Except, we are the underground gone public,
Letting people know what we are doing,
That we stand for the rights of immigrants
To have a decent job and a united family.

*(On occasion of recalling that the 2000 Sanctuary Movement
had its precedence with the El Salvador and Nicaragua civil wars
in the 70s and the Underground Railroad of the Civil War)*

The Wall Without

They built a towering wall to keep a terrorist out—
    Enemy, stranger, rodent, immigrant to rout.
But peace within our walls is the fruit of our labors,
When we interpret the Statue of Liberty to our neighbors.

(On occasion of bringing down the walls within and without)

There Goes Joe

There he goes again
    Forcing himself into our minds
    Like a misbehavin' child in class
    Who becomes obnoxiously
  Intrusive, very public, he is
A personal immigrant crossing my border
    Of propriety,
    But blocking the way as
A John Wayne sheriff in Arizona
    Who is out to corral the alien,
      The invader, the different,
But really hurting, disparaging,
    Spreading hate, splitting families—
He sets the standard for "low" enforcement
    And has urged all of us
    To join him on the border patrol,
So that we feel like spies as one of the posse,
    Cleaning up the tiny laws of pedestrianism,
But the only breakage that needs swept up
    Is the dark dirt of the G.I. Joe patrol.

*(On occasion in 2009 when it would appear that Sheriff Joe Arpaio
is overzealous in law enforcement of immigrants in Arizona)*

Visiting I. C. E.

Seeking place,
    Facing fear
And broken down doors
With big guns and uniforms,
    Capturing immigrants
With provocative ice raids,
That freeze the terror on faces,
    Making everybody terrorists.
The refugee comes
Lost roots,
  Lost to anonymity,
    Lost in a strange land,
Searching for work,
    A place to save their family,
Seeking a place that is safe,
    We need to protest the abuses,
And begin to treat people
    Like real human beings.
We must melt the ice
  And flow like water
    To the river of life.

(On occasion of an action at the place of Immigration & Customs Enforcement
to work out visitation of the detainees)

PART FOUR

Economic Justice

Justice Sides Up with the Poor

.

Lord, when did we see thee hungry or thirsty or a stranger or naked or sick or in prison, and did not minister to thee? Truly, I say to you, as you did it not to one of the least of these, you did it not to me.

MATT 25:44–45

Act Your Wage

Now is the time
    to do the right thing
And support the rights of the needy
By drawing a line on minimal wage
And meeting basic needs for survival.

Being poor
    dehumanizes one's self-esteem,
And sets one off internally as somehow different,
Painfully different when the message of exclusion
Says that some are worth less than a minimum wage.

We need to grow up
    into a just humane society,
By acting our wage, and seeking a living wage
So that we can at the very least free people up
By giving them a chance to stay out of poverty.

(On the occasion of a minimum wage ordinance to go to Kansas City Hall)

Awakened

We feel powerless in the face
    of big bosses,
Which gives power to whoever is in charge,
For fear of punishment, firing and great losses
Because we learn to obey the order of the Sarge.

Perhaps we don't like bosses
    who strut their stuff,

But it will not help to act like a bigger, badder rival,
So we organize our thoughts to face the gruff huff,
By bringing it down to a problem-solving level.
One person enlightened can
      awaken the search.

      Finding two for sanity, support or couple unity,
When joining with three to become like church
Or organizing with four to shape community.

Before you know it, a dozen
      will join a demonstration,
And a Hundredth Monkey will raise the political poll,
To make a quantum leap into moral concentration,
Such that a nation reflects the power of the people.

But it starts one at a time
      when we can say
"We" which allows us to include one more,
And a few less rules and more nurturing our way
So that we can center peace and justice

      at our core.

(On occasion when facing resistance and building a movement is the next step)

Beyond Suicidal Debt

Living beyond our means,
      Is about consumers
Who want to escape to the good life
      And what everybody else has,
Or a nation who wants to pump up
      With the latest military gadget
      While recklessly feeding
The killing machine.

Why are we surprised

When the debt is piled so high
That we all fall down so low,
        And keep doing the same old thing?
Especially when we know how
        To stop unnecessary spending and
        Prevent this suicide escaping.

(On occasion in realizing that consumers are not the only ones spending too much)

Border War

Football.
        Sublimation of aggression,
Or harmless entertainment for war,
        As fans choose sides to

                dominate the foe,
To compete for bragging rights.
        What for?

From football to any game, It's all the same.
        To show whose superior

                in the love of war,
By subjugating a weaker opponent—
We even do it

                with the rich and the poor.

We did it with the Indians,
        took the land,
And we controlled slaves
        and built a cold war wall,
Moving from Viet Nam to Iraq
                with war charades,

Acting like a big Empire,
    only boasting of football.

Yes, football has a problem with all its yelling,
Since everybody is all pumped up
    ready to beat,
Unless you're on the border huddling and
    Wanting both sides to win,

      with no one in defeat.

(On occasion of football between Mizzou and Kansas
and living out the futility of civil war games)

Bottom Line

Corporations use the idea of profits
To motivate their workers
But when profits are not enough
They dismiss their workers.

Corporations like to pretend
That they have more rights than workers
Even refusing tax responsibilities
    To pay their fair share.

If this keeps up, we will hit bottom
And corporations will turn into corpses.

(On occasion of forecasting the recession
contributed by corporations' complicity)

Carelessly Confounded

The money-envied people disconnect,
        Feeling no empathy for suppression,
Seeing the suffering but walking by,
        Schizophrenics in a world of oppression.

Eyes glazed over, they ignore reality,
        Living in a "lahdedah" world of plastics,
Dwelling on the other side of the tracks,
        Protecting a society of consumer monastics.

They may even go to a mega-church
Praying that they are not racists
Even though they participate in a system
        That acts like controlling separatists.

Follow the money into the corporations
        Where assault of workers never stops.
And the rich get richer leaving the poor
        As victims of their games and props.

*(On occasion when the plastic people allow
the take over of corporations which bypass the poor)*

Demythologizing the Politicians

The cry from the skies bounces
        Rain drops off the stubborn ground,
Like all the sorrow of the innocents
        Not penetrating the hard exterior
        Of professional polished politicians.

The stony faces are unresponsive,
        With no more laughter, no tears,
Unable to feel another's pain,
        Hiding behind the rocks
Of insensitive idiotic ideology.

The fraternity of power drunk politicians,
    Enjoying the perks of privilege,
Step over the little people, like smashing
    Anything that's vulnerably weak
    Of apathetic anti-establishment ants.

If only leaders could learn their lessons
    Before it is too late or brings too much damage,
By removing the crunch of competition,
    And causing less suffering to the victims,
By gracing life with a grand gentleness.

*(On occasion when political leaders seem to
lose empathy although there are a few offering hope)*

Entropy

Hoping for a change in Congress,
We wanted to get out of Baghdad,
But the inertia to stay the course
    Drags us down, until we turn
The corner on new bold leadership.
Meanwhile, lives are listless and die.

Until the abomination
    Becomes an Obama nation,
Shaking off all the pit bulls of insurance reform,
    Dragging and clenching his pants.
While the war I.V. stays attached
    And cost overruns could life support
Medicare for all.

*(On the occasion that too much drag from Congress
and the Military Industrial Complex reverses forward progress)*

Just Because

The icon of conservatism—
Milton Friedman—purporting
    Privatization,
    No regulations,
    Small government,
Came up short
    In the Wall St. crisis,
Just like Communism—
Equality for all—
    Doesn't work
In the real world,
    Down went the Berlin wall,
So we live with our limitations,
    Suspecting
That ideals do not fit
    In reality,
Yet, the ideals of Jesus—
To advocate for the poor—
    Still makes better sense,
Rather than the Friedman's
    In the world of walls,
Just because! Of faith!

(On occasion of interpreting conservatism)

Just Doing My Job

Everybody understands, don't they?
That you drop everything
    And make all kinds of excuses,
Because you said the sacrosanct word,
    Let's say it with reverence, "Job."

It doesn't matter what your job produces
Nor the kinds of decisions you make
About peace, justice, and the environment,
Because so many people understand
　　　You are just doing your job.

You can go to work for the nuclear industry
And make lots of money for your family,
And everything will be all right since it is
Not your responsibility to question
Its harm or if it's for the public good,
　　　You're just hired to do the work.

You have the right to take out your mower
And pull out your chain saw
　　　And make all the noise you want
Because everybody understands
You are important as a hard worker
And it doesn't matter that you are disturbing
　　　This writer of this playful tirade
Who prefers leisure and quiet over work.

Now that my neighbor hired workers
To take down a tall majestic tree
　　　Without checking with anyone else—
There goes the neighborhood and the tree
And now I have to glare at my neighbor,
　　　Who was just doing his job
Except it was all right because
　　　He got someone else to do it.

And so you wonder how busy bodies
Keep people from thinking
And questioning the end results
And how much living is depleted
　　　By trying to make a living,
And doing because we avoid asking
What is the purpose of our job?

Do you suppose that God ever wondered
On a Sabbath rest why S/he turned
So much of the work over to humans
Who keep making such a mess of it,
Acting impetuously before thinking,
Because they are just doing their job.

*(On occasion in 2008 of a public hearing when advocates for missile building talked
about jobs and remembering evil events and reasons given—just doing a job)*

Life Savers

The Least of These watch
As the rich boys bail the boat,
Having put holes in the vessel,
Always looking for a hand out
    From those on the shore.

How ironic that instead of helping
    The most vulnerable on the shoreline,
    That perhaps those in the financial Titanic
    Need the most help—not a credit card,
But maybe a "life" preserver.

*(On occasion of the 2008 bailout and Chief Executive Officers
still trying to get big perks)*

Parallels

Historical realities:
    Taking away from the Indians
    By lying and stealing,
Then,
    Israelis taking from Palestinians,
    By occupying their land

And supported by unprecedented US aid,
        Makes you wonder?
Why we need to control?
And why we are silently

            cooperating?
        Parallel disgust!

(On occasion of thinking about the Palestinian plight)

Phantom Wealth

Every time Dow Jones goes up
        The rich get richer, bubbling up
While the poor trickle down,
        Resulting in economic insanity.

We pay the piper for the military,
        And interest on national debt,
We rely on banks to raid the treasury,
        Trading phantom money for real love.

(On hearing that bailouts will save us and wondering
what schemes the rich will pull next)

Return of Sadness

Sadness returns
        When I think about war,
And such a loss
To human life,
        With displaced people

            And empty homes.

Sadness returns
     When I think about people hurting
Because of bills they can not pay,
And the IRS becoming the nation's police
And the homeless begging on sidewalks.

Sadness returns
     When I think about a powerful nation,
Assaulting its own people
With a lack of universal health care,
With a disregard for civil rights,
With a bully attitude over countries,
With exclusion by keeping out immigrants.

But, there is hope,
     When sadness helps us accept reality,
To think more deeply about the meaning of life,
And calls us to right the injustice of all.

(On occasion when disappointments cause a new direction)

Sharing the Pain

Can I see another's pain,
     And not share it too,
Like cold-hearted officials
     Who support the privileged?

How do you pass by
     The Samaritan on the road,
And not feel some guilt,
     Because you can't respond

To every need, so you sift
     Through the mail requests
And toss many in the trash,
     Until you come to the year's end

Categorizing which are important
    That fit your understanding
Of peace and justice, some less
    Supported than tear jerk appeals.

So many needs and so little money
    And time to make a difference,
But you do what you can
    Because you share the pain.

*(On occasion when realizing that overwhelming needs
are not matched by the authorities)*

Taxing

An audit hovers overhead
    Like a vulture ready for food,
That feeds on anxiety instead
    Of what's right and good.

This intimidation is the way
    To keep the poor in line,
So that the military will stay
    And the rich will dine.

Every once in awhile, in due time,
    A war and tax protestor comes along,
    To remind us that we lost the sublime
    And our priorities have gone wrong.

(On occasion when tax resisters are raising the priorities of a nation)

The Bail Out

The wind is shaking the walnuts
    Out of the trees
While fear shakes the money
    From bank accounts.

Since a tornado blew through Wall St.
    While the fat cats scramble for cover,
Because putting the finances together
Exposes the bankruptcy of a system
    Gone amok,
When we pour military expenditures
    Into a huge hole
And the feds keep collecting interest
    Without a care for a final crash,

Well, just a little bit, called a bail out,
And the wind blows
    Over empty promises
    And empty souls
And the poor huddled masses,
Are asleep under the covers,
    Dreaming of a better bail out.

(On occasion of realizing where the real bail out money has gone)

The Flow of God

The cascading water flows around the rocks,
Breathing God's spirit in both rock and water
But more actively seen in the springs of living water,
So where is God?
    In both, but more evident in the water.

So it is we look at the rigid and the moving,
Between the law and the spirit
And we say that we should include both,
Love both, embrace both,
     but side up with the spirit.

Where is it when we look at the rich and the poor?
Do we not say that God gives preferential treatment to the poor?
That is, does not God side up with the poor,
And ask us to stand for social justice
     in the heart of our Exodus.

But no, we state the hypocrisy of loving both sides,
Not admitting that one side has a preference,
As if both are equal…so we find no difference between
The Republicans and Democrats.
     Really now?

If the Republicans were the party to the wealthy,
Would not God be favorable to the party for the poor?
Wait. God loves both Republicans and Democrats,
While always exceptions . . .
     God sides up with the poor.

Rock, water, G.O.P., Demo—
Compassion or social justice,
Both, and, or one over the other?
I'll take a drink of water any day
     before throwing rocks.

(On occasion of analyzing the favor of a God bias)

The Tax Man Cometh

Piles and piles of tax codes
    Have tricked people
Into believing that someone
    Knows what they are doing.
    Sorry, you have been audited,
    And you have been chosen
To play a little complicated game.
    So that everyone will do the same.

(On occasion in 2009 thinking about tax court)

Unbalanced

When nations sleep behind the wheel
    By ignoring the plight of the poor
And leaders pass budgets for an arms deal.
    They damage society, hard to restore.

I wonder how leaders sleep at night,
    When they hurt their own society,
Except maybe they overuse drugs
    To medicate their twisted morality.

America is mentally unbalanced,
    Giving ever more to the rich,
While the impact on our health
    Frantically seeks human attachment.

We must get out of bed with the sleepy rich . . .

*(On occasion of realizing that many politicians are elected because they don't
have a moral compass for the poor)*

Weeping for the Dream

First the government stole land
and moved native Americans

to reservations
Second the government possessed land
and sold African Americans

as property
Third the government globalized
and treated Latinos
as undocumented workers,

sent back when unneeded
Fourth the government excluded
Asians as perpetual foreigners,

unable to have citizenship

So then we perpetuate the myth
That all we have to do is

Work Hard.

But everybody did.

And too many are excluded from the
American dream,

of tolerance for races,
of uplifting the poor,

of settling differences,
of respecting the minority opinion,

of avoiding brutal force.

We can only weep,
And believe,

Nobody is better than another,

but it will eventually get better.

(On occasion when realizing that having the American dream is not enough)

PART FIVE

Passion

Energizing Life

We know that the whole creation has been groaning in travail together until now, and not only the creation but we ourselves, who have the first fruits of the Spirit, groan inwardly as we wait for adoption as sons and daughters, the redemption of our bodies.

ROM 8:22–23

Awesome Autumn

The autumn leaves are aflame
    With the breath of sun,
Dancing a jig in golden dress
    Sparkling in joyous fun.

A few sparse leaves tumble down
    But my gregarious eyes look up
And I feel hope before the winter,
    With just a sip from my coffee cup.

(On occasion when a coffee break breaks the winter war blues)

Brooks Flowing Through

Many are the streams
    Running through our lives
Some which generously flow
    Around the rocks of life,
Others which carry us on like
    Hats on top of the headwinds
Some which race along to give us
    Adventures as fast as the Derby
Others which head us out West
    In open air convertibles and promises
Some which become the delight of food
    Whetting our appetite
Others which turned east to Swaziland
    To nurture children and build schools

The many Brooks connect us as one,
    Leading to a larger ocean,
    Evaporating and raining so as
To grow gardens in our soul.

(On occasion of remembering on July 24, 2007
the effervescent Warren G. Brooks likened to a stream)

Busy Neighbors

Busy neighbors—
    Cleaning house on the outside,
    Running chain saws like vacuums,
    Noisy, thrashing, sweeping,
    Neat and preoccupied,
    So proud of all the accomplishments.
Lying on a hammock—
    I on the other hand doing absolutely nothing,
    So useless, thinking, observing,
    Trees, moving so sexy in the sky,
    Watching a girl and dog—exuberantly greeting,
    Oh, oh—the cicadas sound like chain saws.

(On occasion of watching neighbors and their work ethic
when doing nothing seems just as significant)

Butterfly Leaves

Bountiful butterflies are migrating,
High from the trees they flitter
And sweep across the yard
And ride the wind far from home.

These yellow and orange roamers,
Transformed from lowly buds,
Once gluttonous and deformed,

Fly free and poetic as I want to be.

This doesn't make me want to rake,
Not yet, there is eternity in the skies,
And we must pause and wonder
How such leaves escape their leashes.

And so it goes, as the tree bares itself,
And hope springs for a fruitful time
When the winter empire will be exposed
And replaced by warm summer flowers.

(On occasion of feeling alive in the autumn)

Chasing a Passion for Peace

The light breeze nudges the leaves
        Like a jiggle of bosoms on bare display
Attracting the curious who wonder
        What's behind this passion for life.

Two rabbits flit across the greenly yard
        Hunting a third, raptured in spring fever
And loving the chase for the run of it,
        With the birds and the bees in flight.

Water caresses along rocks of least resistance,
        Settling in pools of deep blue serenity
Calming the restlessness, yet we seek passion
        In a world needy of peace, chasing down rabbits.

(On occasion when the summer yearns to give peace a chance)

Circle of Love

Energy, motion, change—
A wintry retreat quiets the chaos,
Bringing balance to all sides,
Rest and flow, rock and water.

We look for the other path,
More interesting, more alive,
Until we can claim our place,
In the cosmic circle of love.

(On occasion of dynamic tensions embraced by love)

Contributing Forty Years of Love

Two score years ago we scanned the horizon
Looking over the promise
                land of milk and honey
Never fully realizing the challenges
        down the road
But looking back we tasted
        the milk of achievement
Having shared many laps with kids,
                honey sweetened,
Now ready to share a love that is always refreshing
Like streaking sunshine
                after a spring shower,
Like two love birds
        endearing their young.

*(On occasion of officiating at a wedding and anticipating Chicago
at the Drake Hotel marking 40 years of honeymooning)*

Dancing Through the Day

The leaves, green and basking in light
      Flutter in palpitations like flirting girls,
Shifting their hips
      Inviting flying dark peckers to roost
On the nestled folds of their welcoming arms
      Reaching out to embrace
         movement so subtle so alive
that all nature dances away the day.

I join this dance.

It takes me away from the frustrations
      Of the clink clink clink of Wall Street
And the bombastic rat-tat-tat of guns
      And the talk talk talk of lobbyists
        And the chatty cell phone
Interference attacking my gray sanity.

It's summertime. I want a robust dance.

. . . but I would settle for health care.

(On occasion of being upset by the moneyed lobbyists
who are trying to scuttle the single payer idea for health care)

Earth Erected

A light breeze stirs the leaves
      And glances over the earth's skin
As the breath of God caresses
      This bountifully beautiful body—
Love at first sight—awesome!
How I care for this earth erected,
      Intertwined in God's embrace!

(On occasion of coming alive to God's body)

Grasshopper Sex

The green one humped the brown one,
     Clinging piggy back on scrawny legs,
Super glued at the bottom, on a swing set
     Transfixed by our voyeur discovery.

So went the afternoon, rear mounted,
     Not alone, quickly pulsating, pleasuring,
Until another couple came down the path,
     And two lovers jumped like grasshoppers.

(On occasion of experiencing the sexual dynamic in all of creation)

Hand on the Hip

We had been making love for hours,
And could have wrung the sweat from the sheets,
Spent, exhausted,
     panting, throbbing,
Then sabbath rest took over,
     transcending.

Until I put a hand on the hip,
Touching the very place
     where it widens,
Into something full and round and inviting,
Just the idea of it,
     something stirred.

Like filling the valley with the streams,
     Or reaching mountains into the sky,
Or planting seeds in the garden,
     It came like a sacred yearning to complete.

Where does it all come from?
     This need to find significance in another,

With such a desire for filling the gaps,
>   Spreading the natural instinct to procreate.

Ah, overcoming momentary deaths,
>   And snatching aliveness out of the ordinary.
Asserting the courage to be, man erectus,
>   Sliding down the water chute,
>   finally splashing.

Titillated by bare navels alluding to enticing entrances,
>   Like maple helicopters looking
>   for triangular landings,
Like beautiful song birds landing in soft nests,
Plummeting to the depth of an empty void.
To say that one has meaning inside the other.
Giving pleasurable feelings throughout a hot afternoon,
Yields the deepest rest
>   that two humans can ever know,
>   Man and woman entangled
>   in an everlasting embrace.

(On occasion of recreating poetic passion)

Here Walks a Lover

Does the soul know how
>   To make love to God
By expressing outside
>   What convicts us inside?
"Love kindness, do acts of justice,
>   walk humbly in peace."
Then maybe the world will shout
>   That here goes a great lover,
Even, better yet, a lover
>   of creation and
>   a partner for life.

(On occasion in realizing that we are co-creators)

Honeymoons

Let's take a break
     Tasting the memory of love
And dine at the Drake
     For a marriage made from above.

(On occasion of many, many honeymoons)

Life is like a Noisy, Wispy . . .

Released in a half altitudinal way,
It begins with an explosion, phop,
Like sitting on a balloon,
     such a surprise,
One smiles,
     looks around,
And sheepishly walks to
     another space,
Hoping nobody, I mean no body,
     notices
The sweet aroma that penetrates the airways.

So it is, we burst on the scene,
Sometimes wishing we could
     disappear,
Not wanting to embarrass ourselves
By one of life's little oddities—
A poof of the proof and then
     a silent retreat,
As if to proclaim, "Here I am; deal with me!"
And the rest of us suffer
     in wilted resignation.

Life is often like a sneaky fart,
Spread around like fog's
     invisible shadows

Rising to the nostrils of noticeability
But sinking to the depths of impoliteness—
The sign in the diner says,
        "No Farting."
But you might as well say,
        "No Living,"
For we can rely on it, "Death, taxes and farting."

Thus, live with gusto—
        Fart if you must, but discretely.
Permeate the ambience of a room
        With an earthy air of authentic wind.
Excuse me,
        you have a right to be human.
Celebrate your sexy statement of being,
And spread the rumor of your presence,
Lingering in the small chambers
           of public spaces,
You were here,
        you were there,
           everywhere,
Now go away and take some time
        before you visit us again.

        (On occasion in realizing that nobody is better than some body else
                and that we can celebrate our common humanity)

Living the Three Ring Circus

Every man begins center stage
        As close relatives applaud and wow
Every move and twitch and google
        Of the journey from nowhere to now.

And so we take our place in . . . tent,
        To do the work of our significance,

Raising kids and performing a career,
    Showing the world we can dance.

Finally we reside in a side show,
    For freaks of old age keeping any day,
But the grandkids see clowns
    Of silences and wonder and play.

(On occasion of living with passion through all the stages of life)

Pelting Rain

Oh to pause and drink in the sights
Of a shimmering cascade
    Of water splashing
And the greenly glistening trees above
With the infinitely gray elastic skies,
Which invite nature to untangle the knots
Of an uptight world complicated
    By toil and drippy dead ends,
As we slow down and sort out
    What's important
By returning to a natural rhythm
    Even in the drum beat
        Of pulsating rain drops.

(On occasion of experiencing the heart beat of creation through rain drops)

Seven Wives a Week

You are my energizing love, beyond words,
Which cannot contain your multi-dimensionality,
Sinfully, delightfully, poly-married to you
As I reach out to your fascinating personality.

You are my love—first, my Passion Partner,

Who reaches my most intimate desire to seek,
My girl friend, my mistress, my Valentine,
One star, four stars—seven days a week.

You are my second love—a Listening Counselor,
When there are times that the world seems unfair,
And we need the unconditional acceptance—
A healing that comes from someone who will care.

You are my love—my Teacher Preacher Companion,
Who comes alive around children—simply sublime,
Who settled on a vocation to shape minds and hearts
And to change an unaware world one child at a time.

You are my fourth love—a Grand Mother Mentor,
Who produced our wonderful children to enhance
And if nothing else could be an accomplishment,
Then this alone would make enough music and dance.

You are my fifth love—my Chef Creator,
Who is an ultimate connoisseur of a delightful meal,
The one who enjoys wine, chocolate and lobster
And hosts a party that makes everyone squeal.

You are my sixth love—a Leisure Laugher,
Certainly one who is a giggler in the last rest,
That there is more to life than no more monkey business,
That humor is a requirement for life's quest.

You are my seventh love—my Spiritual Mate,
A life affirmer who has brought awareness to the soul,
That we could raise workers for peace and justice
In place of all the forces of war and a misguided goal.

And so love is a myriad of exciting relationships,
Which, I suppose, could be seven mistresses all in one,
And as we look back at our lives, our hearts intertwine.
You, my love, have made this marriage so much fun.

(On occasion of maintaining seven variables through a long term marriage)

Sowing Memorial Ashes

Refrain: "From the earth we come
To the earth we return
In between—we garden."

On this day, marked as Easter,
We come to the garden, not to roll back stones,
But to commemorate this sacred place,
To spread the ashes of Warren G. Brooks.

Ashes, fired and heated after medical research,
But also transforming energy
    Into another form, moving
        From stage to another, requiring work,
        Sometimes, hard work:
To construct change,
        To raise lofty ideas above the trivial,
        To discover the deeper meaning of life,
        To revert the harsh injustices,
            too much and too painful,
        For many victims of unfair practices of greed,
        Pushing their pushiness on others.

But, we wish on this Easter,
        an Alleluia, "Christ is risen Indeed."
To resurrect a hope for living life,
To find humor in its contradictions,
To spot surprising evidence for joy
        in daily adventure,
To spread ashen particles, "blowing in the wind,"
    From our good Fridays into Easter gardens,
        With Eternity all surrounding everywhere…

Refrain: "From the earth we come
        To the earth we return
In between—we garden."

        (On occasion of spreading ashes of Warren G. Brooks
        in the Easter garden on March 24, 2008)

Spark of Hope over Camp Indianola

The morning clouds were gray and dark
    Filled with thoughts of rain and sadness,
When suddenly, surprisingly, a spark of light
    Chastened its beam like a smile across the sea.

(On occasion of attending a same sex marriage in Washington)

Spiraling toward the Center

Hard to do—
    United, to be,
Except, inside you,
    I still can see.

(On occasion of knowing in the Biblical sense)

Stopping Time

Time unrelentlessly rolls on,
    Not stopping to catch its seasons,
Except for a few moments of oasis
    In the desert of meaninglessness.

The best of times can pause,
In the back seat of a Cadillac in Olympia,
    Hidden in a cornfield onto Illinois, twice,
By the tree darkened park of Clinton Lake.

Under the covers of the railway through Montana,
On a truck-swept shoulder of Detroit,
    Dipped in the lake by Sabbatical II,
Cuddled in a gazebo in the back yard.

Skinny dipped by the Lollipop in a Lake Ozark cove,
  Near a sand dune on Pawley's Island,
Dropping an iron at the Tan Tara sixth hole,
Sweating in a Switzerland water closet,

Hoping that one does not get caught,
  Remembering one Tuesday afternoon,
When the first heavenly honeymoon bliss began,
Passionate memories stop
      daily time forever.

(On occasion when slowing time down to Sabbath moments)

The Joy of the Match

Every once in awhile in sports
  One has the chance to be transported
Into a special experience of epic proportion,
  Such was the case of today's
Federer—Nadal tennis match
At Wimbledon, to see the contest,
  Its endurance, the spectacular shots.

Sure it's only a game,
  And both should have won,
Or should not have won,
  Except Nadal luckily edged the other,
And made this game something special.

I was there, giving thanks for
  Witnessing the best game ever.

If only the poor with no TV
Could transcend their lives
  And be something special.

*(On occasion of an exciting 2008 Wimbledon with Nadal triumphing and the
2009 match when Federer and Roddick were so entertainingly competitive)*

The Peace Blessing

You have taught us deep insights,
> When one no longer needs to search
For the attractive, perfect partner,
> But rather to be the real, right person.

You have caused us to listen
> To the message of our hearts,
That life is nurtured through love,
> Gently accepting our humanity.

You have helped us awaken
> To the joy of playfulness,
That we can dance to the heartbeat
> Of waves lapping on the seashore.

You have directed us to the wisdom
> That we need for cooperation,
Rather than competition for success—
> Better when we are contributors of peace.

(On occasion January 23, 2007 when Nia and Katrinka
were sanctioned with a family ceremony)

The Point of Love

If we go to the core of our being,
We can find the energy that will cling to us
> As close as we breathe
> > the great I AM,
Which is love that never departs from us,
No matter if we live or die,
> the I AM is there,
And gives us meaning
> because we yearn

For significance,
    to raise questions about nonbeing
To have the courage to be in the face of nonbeing,
To choose the kind of communities
    that mean everything
That protects us from splitting
        into a thousand pieces,
So that actually we can find peace within.

The above is cloaked with faith
Wrapped up
    in a comforter that calms us,
Even though we experience times
When life disappoints and friends undercut,
And cannot accept the surprise of our being,
    Beautiful, and energetic with love,
Because they are afraid, of change,
    Of times that life is not predictable enough,
That we move through a confusing landscape,
    Lost, but faithful to meeting the I AM
Around the next bend,
    united in this special energy.

There's where the rendezvous will take place
With all kinds of levels of relationships,
    Friends of previous passages, of graduations,
Persons of similar political perspectives,
    Supportive friends through hard times,
Not so close of friends who shared a laugh,
Someone who was a very special God visible,
    And of course, to be married to a close friend makes
    The journey worthwhile,
    validating the point of love.

(On occasion of intersecting God, love, earth, couples, passion)

The Silence of Love

Silences
Between vibrant words,
Jumping across tables
    With animated gusto,
Eyes wide open.
    Eye brows raised
Bouncy breasts,
    And sweeping embraces,
Love sparkles fresh and new
In the beginning,
Until time passes,
    Carelessly,
    Absentmindedly,
And getting laid
    Disappears from the body—
        Never the brain.

(On occasion of seeing passion everywhere)

Turtle on a Log

Turtle on a log
    Basking in the sun
All alone in the pond
    Nothing's done.

Imagine me a turtle
    Hiding in my shell
But sticking my neck
    Out when all is not well.

(On occasion of agitating and risking to go forward)

Umbrella

It feels like rain today,
    Plenty to disrupt plans,
As I look out the window
    I wait for clouds to pass.
My life needs an umbrella
    To find shelter from storms.

I guess I'll stay inside
    And find a place to hide.

Today I will slow it down
    And listen to a sleepy sound.
Splatter, scatter, shatter
    Life goes on Zzzzzzzzzzz.

    Wait, some blue spots appear,
My umbrella turned into a sail.

(On occasion of turning tears into a new energy)

When Down is Alive

Ski in the now and feel alive again,
    Never settling for anything too still,
Or gravity to turn physically heavy,
    Except to speed joyfully down the hill.

When up is down and down is up,
    Time does not wait, resistance is here
Tomorrow is today, in the moment,
    When being up means going down, now.

(On occasion of turning things around and making the best of a situation)

Part Six

Courage

Daring to Do

So we do not lose heart. Though our outer nature is wasting away, our inner nature is being renewed every day.

2 Cor 4:16

1968

        The gods of hope
Walked the earth 40 years ago
        And we mourned their loss
Spilling silent tears on our wilderness
Because of an unrequited love affair
        with an indifferent America.

Some honored its nationalism
        With unbridled, uncritical idealism,
While others loved it enough
        To tell the truth and even
Stroke the underbelly of its violence,
        Guilty of the indigenous genocide
    And the obnoxious tactics of
        Our way or the highway of poverty.

We yearn for the vision of a Bobby,
        A pristine virtue of Jack's Camelot,
        A land of economic and racial justice,
We yearn for M.L.K. Jr., the oratorical resonance
        Of energizing the Constitution,
Rather than being the purveyors of destruction
        And the war criminals of the world,
Reminding us of our legacy
   For peace and justice,
          A kinder and gentler nation.

Forty years of wilderness,
        And still we have no promised land,
So we must retrieve the gods of hope
        And hold them deep inside our hearts,
To turn their vision into ours,

And keep on arriving into the Promised Land.

(On occasion when 1968 was such a pivotal year
and now we open to another pivotal time after 40 years)

A Dream Temporarily Suppressed

M.L.K. called for a true revolution of values,
But not in the sense of accepting any value,
As if we can be lovely dovey with the hate filled,
But instead, values informed by the gospel story,
    In a love for justice
        to restore the soul of America.

A day before he died he was glad to be alive,
Happy not to have sneezed
        at a crazed woman
Who tried to end his life
        with a stab to his aorta,
Since a sneeze would have prevented him seeing
All the progress that begun
        to change segregation.

The sneeze is a sign of a cold in tentative progress,
    Because the next wave of immigration is chilling,
And racism raises its ugly face on the south border,
    While once again the dream of love is only suspended,
Because power and privilege will never kill
        the prophets.

(On occasion of Martin Luther King, Jr.
giving a speech about how close he came to death)

A Half-Masted Patriot Day

Half-masted flags, to remember,
>   The pulverized bodies turned to ash,
Spread everywhere across our 911 memories,
>   Of a horrific day of ghostly pandemonium.

Fear relentlessly visited the soul of Americans,
>   Distracted by the playing of the national anthem,
Saddened, as one, by the direction of history,
>   Society shrunk, cowered and lost its vision.
We voted and elected a boogeyman leader,
>   Who reversed the energy for peace and justice,
Hastening the decline and fall of an Empire,
>   With an avenging war on two fronts—them and us.

Arrogantly, the voices of peace were ignored,
>   Replaced by the strident noise of war,
And pursuit of money and repulsive power
>   Bullied the world into subtle submission.

My tears soak the ashes of another Patriot Day,
>   For I desire a country of a different vision,
One that can bury fear and resurrect some hope,
>   By raising the halyard of justice
>   to fill the sails of peace.

(On occasion when fear rules our memories
and we must take up the call to do better)

A Quick Peek at a War

President lied
People died.

Bullies win
Too much sin.

Compassion lost
War mongers cost.

Masses stand by
Peacemakers sigh.

Prophets spoken
Systems broken.

It's very, very wrong,
Need a new song.

(On occasion to rally a courageous hopeful word)

A Seismic Shift

Most days, life takes one step after another,
    Going in circles leading nowhere much,
Trudging through a war zone of politics,
    Where the knots of existence shut off air.

When suddenly, after an election, breathing deep,
    One shakes off the heavy burden of oppression,
And discovers quick, light steps, turning, turning . . .
    Toward new paths that feel like peace and justice.

(On occasion of feeling relief after an election in 2006)

Agitators

Over a couple hundred years our nation
　　　Began with a quest for freedom, but
A freedom, not so much from tyranny,
　　　As one in which to celebrate agitators, those
Who aspire us to something all we can become,
　　　More than patriots but world citizens,
Courageous agitators for peace and justice for all.

(On occasion of Obama's call to celebrate all that America is on July 4th)

Any Progress after the Wilderness?

Today after forty years when Martin
　　　Delivered his speech at Riverside
We still live in Viet Nam quagmires,
　　　Repeated in Baghdad, showing,
That we never reached beyond the violence.

We talk about a revolution of values,
　　　Cut short, never admitting that the war
Was wrong, and Western arrogance
　　　Would do whatever it wanted to,
For its own profit and control of others.

And the more military defense, bolstered
　　　By fear and ignoring of messy social issues,
We can say with Martin that we have
　　　Approached spiritual death,
Not hostile to poverty and militarism.

We have not changed enough,
　　　And the fear shuts us off from strangers,
And we act tough and as if we are defending
　　　Other people's freedom not to fight,

But we are damaging the gentleness of our soul.

Before we go down, and want to save a vibrant nation,
We call on the transformation of a people,
    To hear the songs of peace,
And be sensitive to those who are in pain,
    To avoid the waste of the future, by caring.

*(On occasion of April 4, 2007 marking 40 years to this day
when M.L.K. delivered his "Beyond War" speech, and was shot down
a year later in 1968, 39 years ago, the same as the length of his life)*

Betrayal

    In the whole range of human experience
Where we see agonizing destruction all around,
And one crazed person can snuff out life,
    Like an arrow into the hart's heart,
    Like a shot toward the playful buoyant bird,
    Like a spear into the free flow of a friggly fish,
So goes the cosmic drama between good and evil,
    Taking and wanting, consuming and killing,
As the Godses assassinate the non-violent Gandhi.
And the Booths of the world take out the Lincolns,
And the Oswells sneak attack a Pres. John Kennedy,
And the Sirhans lower the vision of Bobby Kennedy,
And the Rays shut the voice of Martin Luther King, Jr.
And the Carl powerbodies silence the vision of any minister,
    Then there are Judas nobodies who thwart Jesus' ministry,
        What betrayals, what sadness, what sacrifices,
Yet the truth lives,
    the spirit survives,
        the love endures,
And in the whole range of things God's grace is still there,
Whether we leave the earth early or late,
        the light flickers
    Still the same, the light last forever.

(On occasion of seeing the last day of Gandhi at the Kansas City Fringe Festival)

Beyond Crucifixion

Easter people learn to live in a Good Friday world,
    Where deceit, harsh words, pain, mobs, violence,
   back-stabbing, disappointment, torture, injustices, and lies
create the conditions for depression and hypocrisy,
While only a people with Easter eyes
    can end this despair
        and see beyond the current reality.

(On occasion of seeing the value of faith)

Birth Sounds

Eight square and many days ago,
    I was placed on this planet earth,
Not on my own accord but because,
    Something transcends my birth.

The significance of which I am still
    Playfully and humorously working out,
Never to retire from prophetic voices,
    From sabbatical silence into a Shalom shout.

(On occasion of not giving up on birthdays)

Butterfly Jitters

Most people are clueless
    On political and religious issues
Until something shakes their ideas
    Risking a cross to the other side,
Turning from cocoons into butterflies.

(On occasion that all can change using the butterfly metaphor)

Cockadoodle

Cockadoodle, cockadoodle, El Presidente,
    The little banty rooster struts his stuff,
Reversing everything dear to one's heart
    And turning backward the word *live*.

How could a nation have sunk so low
    With the lies, the debt, the killings, the waste,
The hypocrisy, the suspicions, the gaps
    In a nation that has tarnished its democracy.

Never should conservatives seek leadership,
    Since they're only good at reacting to liberals,
And find their identity through critiquing change,
    And secretly plotting to be boastful superheroes.

And now thirty-five articles of impeachment
    Were presented for the congressional record,
Which is a witness to how much has gone wrong,
    And shows that pride often goes before the fall.

May a nation go to its knees and stand again,
    More humbly, more penitent,
        more humane,
    Less ready to use military force, less greedy,
More concerned about a world
        getting along.

*(On occasion around June 12, 2008 when Chavez
referred to a U.S. President as the "Li'l Gentleman")*

Dance Then Wherever You May Be

Anywhere you stand around the world,
    You look up at the day sun and night stars,
Feeling elated with hope and lightness,
    That life is the experience of a new dance.

Wandering forty years in the wilderness,
    With a brief oasis of a Carter or Clinton,
But thirsty to drink in a Kennedy's Camelot,
    We can enjoy Obama's historic moment.

He wanders into the raging storms,
    Seeking the still waters of peace,
Cupping his hands by opening his fist
    To pour refreshing water over our eyes.

We can move out of our sleepiness,
    To come awake for daring dancing,
And become points of cosmic energy,
    To embrace a movement for justice.

(On the occasion of Obama's Inauguration)

Disappointment

Every leader knows
    The hurt of powerful forces
        Taking down a good idea
When you stew on what it
            could have been

A progressive leader who cares
        Is sensitive to criticism
But sometimes one compromises
    Too much of the right thing,
    Just to keep a job
        Or to be liked,
        Or to wait another day
        And when you face life's hardness,
        A health issue,
        A faith value versus militarism
        A job that pays the bills

rather than feeds the soul,
you accept the contradictions between
    being and nonbeing
    faith and creatureliness
    a higher call or the easiest way
    speaking out or being afraid
    not yet or already here

But I would never never never
    Be disappointed if my daughter
Did not marry a Baptist or Republican,
I mean bless them for they can be loved
    But you just have too much drag,
Too much singing of
        "We shall overcome."

(On occasion of wondering how often leaders disappoint by not adopting their crisp campaign promises because ruling boards pull vision back into mediocrity)

Grandson

Your grand entrance
    Brings joy to my heart
Palpitating to beats
    Of a different drummer,
For I will march to music
    That sees hope-filled joy
And works for justice
    And walks gently on the earth,
And tolerates persons along the path,
    To become the most authentic
        Expression of human love.
This is my prayer of peace for you.

(On occasion when Isaac Alexander Faust came into the world since every occasion of birth offers hope for a different world)

Grave Defiance

Up from the grave I got up,
Unyielding. Defiant, Alone, Never
Will I go to my grave as a sham,
But will turn the light on
      to see through the darkness.

Rejecting,
      When war is peace,
      The idea that taxes are mandatory,
      And any effort of the government
            to tyrannize
            "We the people"
            with evasive policing
            and snooping
            and using force
            to intimidate.
Resisting,
      Corporate snobbery,
      Wealthy profit grabbers,
      Environmental abusers,
      And purveyors of I.D. cards
            and spy chips.

I will not go gently into my grave
      by simply submitting,
If I must give into bullying,
      Disrespect of workers, all kinds,
      And shutting out the least of these,
Who shine the light of authentic humanity.

      No . . . I stand,
            for justice of all
      And for our diverse selves, yet to come,
            and free to be you and me.

(On occasion of defying death and insignificance)

Holiday Hope

Tis the season for Christmasbility,
    When the seriousness of duty and darkness
Turns into a lightness and carefreeness
    Where love fires up joy and sparkiness.

Every person needs an absolution
    Of those things that keep us down
And once a year we can let go of the past
    And feel free enough to sing a new sound.

Come into our lives and refresh the truth
    Removing the despair of deceitful leaders
To be replaced by capable, courageous poets
    To issue in peace and justice as our greeters.

(On occasion of calling for a new day)

Hope for Half a Century

Not since John Kennedy have we seen
    The promise of poetic language
And oratorical skill that raises the horizon
    Of a new era, a new hope, a better day,
Since the Obama surge is passing the energy
    Onto a populace who have been oppressed
By a half a century of frustration and struggle
    Under the weight of hypocritical politicians,
Alas, we feel a relief from the war enforcers
    And enter
        a revolution in uplifting humanity.

(On occasion for appreciation of poetic language to raise our spirits)

If Only

The birth of Isaac Faust laughs and
      Brings much hope in a 911 world
When on September Ten
      We did not have the fear,
      And the revenge of "them first,"
      And let's go to war and make money,
No, if only it had turned out differently,
And we could nurture the development
      Of human potential and newness,
And the cosmic significance
      Of a beloved, "wanted" child.
That beloved, wanted
         child should be peace.

(On occasion of the birth of Isaac September 10, 2008 to change the "if" in life)

Misguided Media

Television reports the negative,
      And when an issue comes up
Stations look for an opposite slant,
      So the right receives hot air time.

Something in the news is missing,
      More than just a dichotomy of views,
Something about what informs
      The clarity of a minority perspective.

The popular position of a nation,
      Ready to defend itself from enemies,
Finds support from the media,
      When deeper truths need to be told.

(On thinking about how the media got it so wrong about the Iraq war)

Newsworthy Noise

Today we commemorate the forgotten ones,
    Those who silently died outside of fame,
Who projected a gentle spirit, quiet
    And peaceful, not seeking attention, yet
Offering an authentic and humble humanity.

No, they are not the ones who aggressively
Attack others and victimize the helpless,
Who go to war to defend their honor,
Who try to out-compete rivals and enemies,
    All in the name of their own significance.

Those who use force and are so certain
Of their conservative point of view,
The sleepy ones who lie, comforted by the flag,
They are the attention getters of a younger age,
Who take up everybody's time, the teachers,
The reporters, who record those who stir the noise.

Thus, this pro-war world is busily chaotic,
    Demanding to be counted and noticed,
And the killing and destruction persists,
    With the pricey pursuit of power and prestige,
But it is in the forgotten ones who dip deep
    Into the well of grace and peacemaking—refreshingly,
These are the promised voices who will last eternally.

(On wondering where the real news is and who notices the forgotten heroes)

No More Silence

Those in power will use
    Every means to keep it,
Even if it means deceit, lies,

Bribes, killing, revenge,
Every value that looks evil,
 Because it wants to win.
 To confront this blind power
 Requires organizing actions
That will change the world
 From destruction to love—
Take heart, courageous partners,
 We will rise to speak to power.

(On occasion of moving to a higher calling)

Obama Kool-Aid

An Obama revolution for real,
But does a movement for electability
And electricity need corporate marketability
 Without selling our soul to its control?

 We want Obama without the Kool-Aid
By listening to his progressive constituency,
 Who will only pay the piper when
He counters corporate irresponsibility.

We need to take on the gilded rich,
 By elevating policies of peace and justice
 That stand with the basement people,
And reverse the destruction of the greedy.

The American psyche is full of Kool-Aid
 And devoid of values, when you need oil,
Then take it, no matter the ecology costs,
 When will we ever ever
  never never learn?

*(On occasion of putting a lot of hope in leadership
but recognizing some of the limitations to this leadership)*

Obama Phenom

The Obama Phenom creates a movement
    Surging with synergy and buoyant with hope
Turning the despair of war and imprisonment
    Into a higher vision to once again cope.

(On occasion of recognizing new energy to the struggle)

Obama Shama

How refreshing the flow of a speech
    Before the congress and American people
That actually has a vision that would teach
    And raise one's sight toward the steeple.

*(On occasion of President Obama's first address to congress on February 24,
2009 laying out goals to address the economic crisis.)*

Ode to a Fellow Peacemaker

Once a fellow peacemaker took a shortcut to heaven,
    Pretty much unrecognizable, the name with the face,
So I wondered if peacemakers make a difference
    Or if we just fail to appreciate another's gift of grace.

And so we come and go weaving our particular
    Web of intrigue, sometimes catching life
And other times missing so much of its awesomeness,
    Wondering if death is the only peace from strife.

Maybe peacemakers are like insurgent poets,
    Irrelevant, dissident, disregarding the status quo,
    Imagining a vision of a world that gets along
When "staying the course" is not the way to go.

Yet people of faith keep on this unknown journey,
        Because of the conviction that the value of peace
Is worth every passion, more precious than gold,
        And like seeds of a garden,
                its fruits will increase.

*(On occasion of a tribute to Kansas City American Friends
Service Committee Director Ira Harritt on September 8, 2007)*

Overwhelming

Having too many options,
        And too many good causes
Spin the energies
        Into an overwhelming vortex
Of unsuccessful ventures.

        All I've got to do is dive in!
But first I've got to get the feet wet.
Wait, maybe it's the mind to focus in,
        What's important here? See,
Oh, my, it's overwhelming.

Peace, Justice,
        A little bit of that, scattered,
And if we save the world,
It will be in spite of ourselves,
And finding a bit of the plan,
        To do what we think is right.

(On occasion of realizing that a person can't do everything)

Pancake Religion

Sometimes religion gets too syrupy
      Too sweet too pious
Too flat to consume adult portions
      As it loses its well-roundedness
And leaves out whole chunks
      Of how to find justice for neighbors,
By turning in on itself as oppressors,
      Perhaps hastening its own demise,
With trivial pursuits of end times.

This popular buffet of religion and fear
may hold the secret ingredient
      for a new batch of Kool-Aid.

*(On occasion of thinking about the Kansas City Star's front-page coverage
of the International House of Prayer, which seems to be
the latest herd instinct of religion looking for signs of the times)*

Picking up the Mess

Why can't peace move as quickly
      As violence destroys,
And see that the destructiveness of a nation,
      Only promotes the crisis,
By continual fighting with a phantom enemy,
      Accusing others of being naïve in the ways of war.
And so all the worse values are enhanced,
      And all of us go down, free falling in shame,
Because drunken leadership is in a downward spiral,
      Helpless until the country hits rock bottom.

Coming to terms with our destructive approach
      By avoiding the nurture of communities
      And recovering community values,

Recognizing interdependence,
And attachment to the earth
      And rediscover what it means to be human
And shift off of slavery and inequality,
By discovering a whole set of nurturing, finding
      What is best in us, not what is worse.

People rush around, destructive in their behavior,
      Not thinking about where it is all headed,
Delaying the more important things,
      Until they confront a deadline,
And look for relief from the crisis.
Problem is that too many crises pile up,
And we look for a rescuer rather than
      Take personal responsibility to problem solve.
We have made such a mess, all preventable,
      That we wait for the next messiah.
But we wait too long, and we are the ones
  Who need to get up
      and be nudged into the answer,
And start picking up the mess.

(On occasion in deciding what we can do instead of not doing anything at all)

Playing a Poetic Part

The lyrical voice of a poet ebbed into silence
      As pain subsided and eased into a cosmic grace
And her shriveled carcass was tossed into a box
      But echoes of a rhythmic song came from a far place.

It's in a word, a phrase, that energizes our soul
      Which gives us hope facing the glimpses of death,
In which we tap an inexhaustible promising word
      To face the fragile journey and take the next breath.

Moving through the years as a poet magnetized
    A path to her doorstep, to entertain with elegance,
From the poor to the rich, of citizen and President,
    Each honored as a guest, treated with awe and dance.

She will remind us that kind words are a lovely art
    That softens too much hurt in this world of sin,
Because we can set our sights on higher things
    By using the wisdom and care of a renegade pen.

Such a poet brought out the inner beauty in all of us,
    So that we felt better in the presence of a gentle heart,
And we could enter the fray for peace and justice
    By listening to her legacy and doing our poetic part.

*(On the occasion of a Memorial Service
on January 4, 2008 for 102-year-old poet Viola Zumault)*

Redressing the Egregious

A steady rain pats the swollen ground
    As often as votes click the ballot box
To mark the passage of political seasons
    When leadership inspires energetic talks.

Down, down, down we fell into a dirty war,
    That reflects the lowest of human behavior
And the destruction of a nation's tarnished spirit
    Which ignores the higher values of our Savior.

We can no longer hide behind the hypocrisy
    Of a nation that puffs up law and order
By using military force to terrorize people
    And scapegoat our problems to the border.

We are looking for a new day and a new hope
    When people might raise their sensitive sights

Beyond their undeveloped, imprisoned answers
    To claim more open, liberal, progressive rights.

        (On occasion when many are looking for a better day)

Reimagining Peace

Ever since the tower in Iceland
    Shot six beams of light into the sky,
Once again we imagine the possibility,
That peace could come to you and I.

Oh of course peace is a distant dream,
    With all the bullyness of the world,
But John Lennon gave us a song of hope,
  "Imagine Peace"–give it a twirl.

        (On the occasion of the dedication of the Imagine Peace Tower
        on October 9, 2007 in Iceland)

Reinventing America

America owns the world,
So it seems, it doesn't matter
    What other "unpeople" think.
Because if they dislike our rules,
Too bad, it doesn't count,
Since we call the shots our way,
    As long as we get the oil
        In exchange for our guns
        or by extra friendly persuasion.

Selling war is like selling cars,
With a little snake oil thrown in
Plus a push of patriotism

Into a gas tank
    Of ill-conceived ideas
    And huge dreams of money
Until you drive like crazy
Right into a dead end street.

This pell-mell road to destruction
Is like so many things that go wrong
Since it subtracts from our potential
And diminishes our energy
Except for one thing, the human spirit
Can survive the worst of times
By not going alone, greedily, rather,
    Reinventing a better tomorrow
    And joining the world community.

*(On occasion of seeing a government's propensity
for destruction and it doesn't even realize it)*

Sabbatizing Salaam

Shalom, Salaam, Peace,
Sabbatize us in your vision of peace,
Where we no longer justify our conflicts,
    Torture, and meanness to our enemies,
But that we turn from destruction, fear
    And resolve war with the energy of love,
By courage within we work for justice
    And building up a new, different creation.

(On occasion of catching a basic value that drives us)

Shalom Zone

I yearn for the leaping greenly leaves teasing
    My sensibilities
And the blue sheets of sky covering
    My comfortable hide-away,
But I long for the energy
    To fight the dragons of death
        And the shadows of injustice,
To dream and create a universal shalom zone.

(On occasion for the courage to be in the right place)

Silence the Violence

I like this phrase,
    Silence the violence,
If only we could reach
Such a day of balance.

All around us we see
Violence with our words
And forcing others by laws
To constrain them into herds.

I guess the anger is so loud
    That it doesn't listen to love
And the fear is so strong
    That we can't hear what's above.

(On occasion of curbing the violence in our lives)

Songs of Commitment

Repetitive refrains are annoying
Especially when they trivialize life
And promote feelings over thinking,
As people walk in a trance through strife.

How will we take responsibility
For reforming Washington and Wall St,
As long as we build walls that suppress
The song that makes us most complete.

    We have got to listen to the music
Of our soul but move beyond sentiment
    To the great voices of peace and justice
So we can engage in a deep commitment.

(On occasion of using the music of our generation
to abate the cruelty of the world)

Sorting through the Hypocrisy

The less you know
    The more certain you can be,
    About guns and country, or
Bullying, money, power, control, force,
    Conservative, tradition, patriotism,
    Empire, fighting, corporations.
Does this sound like a formula for change,
    Or is it more of the same?

So why would you raise value questions
    Unless you conclude that wisdom
Comes from questioning all these values,
    Before we can have peace, justice,
Openness, ecology, tolerance,

And authentic expressions of love.
> The choice is ours.

We are the ones to find
> What's really real,
> And what's below the surface,
Sorting through the hypocrisy
> To express genuine values
> For a kinder and gentler world.

> *(On occasion in discerning the significant values)*

Spring Cleaning

Spring cleaning, house parties, thrift stores,
> Are good preparation for busy seasons,
To start over, to get organized, to remove
> The bloody grime
> > under our nation's fingernails.

> *(On occasion of having the courage to keep at it)*

Stirred Up

Storms stir the stillness,
The chimes clang,
> The wind howls,
The birds bounce off twigs,
> And trees hover in the cold.

Storms stir the soul,
Inside I shake,
> I cry for no war,
And the Bush Presidency covers his ears,

Blurs his vision,
Smirks a quivering smile,
Blowing off the lint of criticism,
But the other storm knows how to end,
While my rage stirs that part of me that refuses
To believe that we were meant to live
From one storm to another.

(On occasion of realizing that storms are a part of life and cause us to act)

Stop the Madness

This madness must cease,
So cautioned Martin Luther King
In his speech "Beyond Vietnam"
But how will we go beyond Iraq?
Unless we cease the madness,
And allow love to be the last word.

(On occasion to wonder why we keep going from war to war)

Take Aways

Some are mistakenly perceived as change agents
When what they do is look at what's there,
Finding ways to destroy or dismantle an idea,
Reversing all the good reasons that made it fair.

Rather than create new ideas and move forward,
We have all these people who want to step back,
But I wonder how we will ever gain any progress,
Knowing that myopic vision is due to a blurred cataract.

No longer can I subtract and call it positive change
   If things like affirmative action and civil rights
Took so much energy to achieve their acceptance,
   Then what we need is new changes in our sights.

(On occasion to ask for better eyesight and a bigger vision)

Take Courage

The way is often hard,
The path has many unknown detours,
   Some which reveal another truth,
But which may open many more doors.

*(On occasion to keep peeling away the layers
and develop a more courageous truth)*

The Oxymoron of a Good War

War unlocks the killing machine,
Destroying people and breaking things,
Bringing home these acts of destruction,
Its medals can not be glorified as "Good."

So the world is attracted to war,
Infusing power and energy and patriotism
For the bully heroes who wish to do
Damage and smell blood of the other side.

The memory of war does not erase
The emotion of killing before being killed,
So the raw edges open up wounds
Unhealed by the hypocrisy of "goodness."

The pain is so deep and horrid,
Suffering from our myths about W.W.II,
Thinking that all subsequent wars
Must eliminate Hitler's image.

We need more prophetic peacemakers,
Learning creative ways to speak the truth,
And bring repentance to the awful wrong
We spend on war rather than on children.

(On occasion of breaking the myth of war)

The Reading of U.S. Poet Laureate Don Hall

The Poet was led slowly to a table,
     Quietly listening to all the accolades,
And bemused by the awe of the audience,
     Who came to hear a disheveled old man.

He slowly paged through his book of poetry,
     As his faltering voice fell into a rhythmic,
Sonorous drone that lulled one close to sleep,
     To dream that everyone could became a poet.

Maybe he had not worked a day of his life,
     Which is not far-fetched if you love your work,
Because what touches the heart is pleasurable,
     And poetry is wondrously close to making love.

If only we could use the imagination of the poet,
     And go beyond the distractions of daily chores,
Moving ahead of the old ways of thinking,
     Beyond the prisons of war and hate and divisions.

(On the occasion of Don Hall at Rockhurst in 2007)

The War Room

When you tiptoe quietly, pass the room,
In order not to disturb or be disturbed,
You save your hide from a tongue thrashing,
As Elders sip red wine over whispered plans.

Making plans about collateral damage.

You imagine what it would be like to burst
Into the room and say, "Just a moment.
Are you sure you want to make plans to kill?"
Only dreaming, as they escort you away to be interrogated.

But not yet; you still have your job.

They explain it to you again, again, and again,
"We have to defend our country from our enemies,
And those who do, have a chance to die with honor,"
And when they say this, they seem convinced.

You're not.

Probably not, because no matter how you dice it,
War is wrong—so is killing, so is stealing,
So is lying, but who cares about that,
It's just the best way to defend yourself.

You're not convinced.

You look down, cut, red is dripping from your hands,
If only you could have said something,
If only you could have done something,
The drones have bombed innocent victims.

You were too quiet.

> *(On occasion when you learn that ordinary family men go to work and
> routinely drop bombs on civilians and you don't know what to do about it)*

The Weaning of Amy Goodman

Never. My life has gone static
    Like the radio station that droned on
Leaving me unconscious of Amy,
    With nothing to think about,
Cutting my heart like a buzz saw.

Amy is the corpuscle that attacks
    The germ of right wing Christian hate,
And feeds my humanness
    So I can join others
With a similar heart condition.

(On occasion when a station didn't program Amy Goodman)

The Winds of Change

As the wind blows
    Over the golden leaves
A new stirring is in the air,
    Where compassion is spread
Where money is shared
    Where health care cares
And the cost of war is shifted
    Over to the care of people,
A new stirring is moving
    Through the voting booth.

(On the occasion when the pendulum swing of voters expects a new energy)

Wise Journey of Tomas Young

orry to hear you have fallen into a coma,
blood clot from your arm found the lungs,
And has attempted to silence your voice,
ur "body" of war will not go quietly,

ger could I abstract about the reality of war
For you challenged all my preconceptions,
othing was left of the empty rhetoric
That war falsely drives our energy for life.

litary madness was trumped up by slogans,
aq would use weapons of mass destruction,
ey were the aggressors, terrorists ready to attack,
That we only need to trust our leadership who knows best.

ard it in Vietnam, though Iraq is not the same,
same reasons are given, that so many die,
ring how many it takes to come to our senses
From this insanity that 911 gave us a license to kill.
We wrote a blank check after 911 with no financial limits,
e we were going to get the monkey off our back,
to be crippled by the Viet Nam syndrome,
e would win democracy for Arabs at all costs.

fell into a coma, this cheerful American innocence
That would have us go shop rather than deal with death,
And live with hypocrisy rather than examine the truth,
pt the razzle dazzle rather than to be awakened.

for being astutely aware when it counted,
ving voice to the wounded and the war victims,
ing a soldier who brought an alternative to killing,
real hero, wise in consciousness on an endless journey.

(On occasion of the extraordinary courage of an Iraqi Peace Vet
who would be consigned to a wheelchair for life documented
in the film "Body of War" on June 11, 2008)

To Die with Honor

To die with honor,
      Or to do what is right,
Better to protest with courage,
      And honorably avoid a fight.

                    (On occasion to change the formula for patriotism)

To Do Peace

To do peace
      While living in a pro-war world
takes courage to absorb the aggressive
      shock waves of brainwashed,
            patriotic, fearful people,
and transform them into more gentle
      reactionaries—to be peaceful,
not by force but by nurturing peace.

                    (On occasion to ask who has the real courage)

Two Steps

One step forward, two steps back,
      Any progress seems formidable,
Some love the "shock and awe" of war,
      Only a few put the broken pieces together again.

From Omar Torrijos to Roldos,
      from Arbenz to Mossadegh,
from Allende to the nameless whose lives
      Are cut short by the corporatocracy.
From Johnson to Nixon,
      From Carter to Reagan,

Clinton to Bush—
Once hope, easily dashed!

The new slave traders appear overseas,
Disguised as corporations hiring desperate people
Are simply trying to take care of their families,
Looking for a chance to free themselves from poverty.

Prophets disappear, and the bullies take over,
Until enough people can't take it anymore,
Change the stranglehold of corporations,
Hoping for two steps forward, only one step back.

I, at last, take two steps, there's Obama.

(On the occasion of despair unless we have a new surge of hope)

alizing Where

les dream of a world where every person is
Perceived as a child of God—dignified, respected—
no person is seen as better than another,
g strategies to overcome violence,
hering around the open table of Sabbath rest,
nect with other persons caring about the earth,
Not taking from but creating a better place,
courageous persons speak out for peace,
Embracing pluralism, transcending nationalism,
persons work for justice,
all kinds of work is valued and compensated fairly,
Where the poor and oppressed get a fair shake,
Where all rise to become more kind, gentle
and loving, transforming our neighbors.

casion of a Disciples Peace Fellowship meeting on April 20, 2009 to make
a statement on "What would a world of justice and peace look like?")

Vote Out Insidious Piggy Backs

Congress creeps on the dark side
      By sliding violence into our sanctuaries
And falling into the slimy pit of compromise

    Outrage to the clarity of ideals
That shuns creativity and elevates
      Weapons of destruction,

How low and brutish must leaders become,
      Unless we hear from forgotten throwaways
Who care to be accountable for the people.

For they are the voice that Congress must hear from,
      Against violence, the gun madness must stop,
And concealed weapons must be checked at
The door of our happy-triggered senators.

*(On occasion when Congress attached a rider about guns
in national parks onto a credit card bill on May 27, 2009)*

Watermelon in the Sky

I looked up to my left, high,
      Unbelievable to what I have seen
A watermelon in the sky,
Lying on its back, partly eaten.

I suppose it would be more exact
To say that I saw a glimmering moon,
      Imagine—if I could reach this snack,
I would take a bite—right soon.

each up to tip its end,
d see-saw a white watermelon,
uld suck its seeds to send
t solutions to every war I spit on.

(On an occasion of whimsicalness which may be the only
courageous thing to do in the face of the seriousness of the situation)